THE WONDERS OF THE RAINFOREST

A KID'S GUIDE TO AN AMAZING ECOSYSTEM

BRIAN THOMAS

CONTENTS

INTRODUCTION

Rainforests are called "rain" forests for a good reason. They're some of the wettest places on the planet! Rain can fall almost every day in some of these forests, which helps keep them lush and green. All that water and warm weather create the perfect environment for plants and animals to thrive. Think of it like a massive greenhouse, except this one is natural and filled with wild surprises.

But what exactly *is* a rainforest? It's more than just a forest that gets a lot of rain. A rainforest is a special type of ecosystem—a huge community of plants, animals, and other living things all working together to survive. These forests are found near the Earth's equator, where the sun shines bright and the weather stays warm year-round. There are two main types of rainforests: tropical and temperate. Tropical rainforests, like the famous Amazon, are warm and located near the equator. Temperate rainforests are cooler and found in places like the Pacific Northwest of the United States.

What makes a rainforest different from, say, the woods near your house or the forests you might see on a hike? For one, rainforests are *dense*. That means they're packed full of plants—so many that sunlight barely reaches the ground in some places. You could walk through the rainforest and barely see the sky because of the thick canopy of trees overhead. This canopy isn't just a roof of leaves; it's a whole world of its own. Birds, monkeys, and insects live high up in the trees, where they find food, shelter, and safety.

Below the canopy, there's another layer called the understory. It's darker and cooler here, and plants with big leaves grow to soak up the little sunlight that sneaks through. Animals like jaguars and snakes might prowl in this shadowy layer, blending into the greenery. Finally, at the very bottom is the forest floor. This layer might seem quiet compared to the buzz and chatter above, but it's just as important. The ground is covered with fallen leaves, plants, and rotting wood that break down into rich soil. This soil feeds the trees and plants, creating a cycle of life that never stops.

Rainforests are home to more living things than any other place on Earth. From the tiniest ants to towering trees that are hundreds of years old, everything in the rainforest plays a role. You might think of the rainforest as a giant puzzle, where each plant, animal, and insect is a piece that keeps the whole thing working. If one piece disappears, it can affect everything else. For example, some trees rely on bats to spread their seeds. Without bats, those trees might not grow, and the animals that depend on those trees for food or shelter would have a harder time surviving.

One of the most fascinating things about rainforests is their diversity. Diversity means there are lots of different types of plants and animals living together. Scientists estimate that rainforests are home to more than half of the species on Earth, even though they only cover about 6% of the planet's surface. That's like cramming more than half of all the world's animals and plants into a space smaller than the state of Alaska!

Picture this: a single rainforest tree might hold hundreds of species of insects, some of which scientists have never even seen before. That's right—there are animals and plants in the rainforest that humans are still discovering today. It's a bit like exploring a treasure chest where every item is unique, valuable, and full of surprises.

The plants in the rainforest do more than just look beautiful. They also help the planet in ways you might not expect. Many of the medicines people use come from rainforest plants. Scientists have studied plants in these forests to create treatments for diseases like cancer and malaria. Every time a new plant or tree is discovered, it could hold the secret to curing a disease or solving a problem we haven't even thought of yet.

Rainforests also help keep the Earth's air clean. Trees and plants absorb carbon dioxide, a gas that contributes to climate change, and release oxygen into the air. In fact, rainforests produce about 20% of the world's oxygen. Some people call them the "lungs of the Earth" because of this important role.

But rainforests aren't just about trees, animals, and cool weather. They're also full of incredible sounds. Close your eyes and imagine listening to the rainforest. You might hear the deep croak of a frog, the chatter of monkeys swinging through the trees, or the steady hum of insects. Each sound tells a story about life in this unique place. It's a constant symphony, where every creature has its part to play.

Life in the rainforest isn't easy, though. Plants and animals have to adapt to survive. Some animals, like sloths, move slowly to avoid being noticed by predators. Others, like poison dart frogs, use bright colors to warn enemies that they're dangerous. Even the plants have their tricks. Some grow sharp thorns to protect themselves, while others produce chemicals to keep hungry animals away.

Rainforests are also full of mysteries. Scientists believe there are still thousands—maybe even millions—of species living in rainforests that we haven't discovered yet. What if the next big discovery is hiding high in the canopy or deep in the shadows of the understory? It's exciting to think about all the secrets these forests might hold.

Where are rainforests found in the world?

Close your eyes for a moment and picture Earth as it might look from space. You can imagine the swirls of blue oceans, the white streaks of clouds, and the patches of green that cover parts of the land. Those green areas are where life is thriving—and some of the greenest, most alive places are the rainforests. But rainforests aren't everywhere. They exist in very special parts of the world, in areas that have just the right combination of heat, sunlight, and rain to keep them bursting with life.

Rainforests love the heat, and they love water, which is why most of them are found near the equator. The equator is an invisible line that runs around the middle of our planet, like a belt. It's the warmest part of Earth because it gets the most direct sunlight all year long. If you were to travel along the equator, you'd find that it passes through countries with some of the most famous rainforests on the planet—places like Brazil, the Democratic Republic of the Congo, and Indonesia.

Let's start in South America, home to the Amazon Rainforest, the largest rainforest in the world. The Amazon is absolutely enormous—it's bigger than the entire country of India! It stretches across several countries, including Brazil, Peru, and Colombia, and it's so dense with trees and plants that it creates its own weather. Seriously. The trees release water into the air, which forms clouds, and then those clouds bring rain. It's like a natural recycling system for water. The Amazon is also home to countless animals, from sloths to jaguars to brightly colored parrots. It's a place where life thrives in every direction you look.

Now imagine crossing the Atlantic Ocean to Africa. There, you'd find the Congo Rainforest, the second-largest rainforest in the world. It's spread across countries like the Democratic Republic of the Congo, Gabon, and Cameroon. The Congo Rainforest is filled with towering trees, winding rivers, and animals like gorillas and forest elephants. Unlike the Amazon, which has mostly flat land, the Congo Rainforest has rolling hills and even some mountains, giving it a slightly different personality.

Keep traveling east, and you'll reach Southeast Asia, where rainforests are scattered across countries like Indonesia, Malaysia, and Thailand. These rainforests are a bit different because they're often connected to islands and coastlines. They're famous for their orangutans, tigers, and incredible plants like the rafflesia flower, which is the largest flower in the world. Some of these rainforests even extend into the ocean, blending into mangrove forests that protect the shores from storms and provide homes for fish and crabs.

If you journey further east across the Pacific Ocean, you'll discover smaller rainforests on islands like Papua New Guinea and Fiji. These rainforests might not be as big as the Amazon or the Congo, but they're just as fascinating. Because they're on islands, they're often home to animals and plants that exist nowhere else on Earth. Imagine walking through one of these forests and spotting a bird or a tree that no one has ever seen before—it's the kind of place that feels like a real-life treasure hunt.

But rainforests aren't just tropical. There's another type called temperate rainforests. They're found in cooler places but still need lots of rain to survive. One of the most famous temperate rainforests is in the Pacific Northwest of the United States, stretching through parts of Washington, Oregon, and British Columbia in Canada. Instead of monkeys and parrots, you'd find animals like black bears, deer, and spotted owls here. The trees in temperate rainforests are often covered in moss, giving them a magical, fairy-tale-like appearance.

It's incredible to think about how these rainforests are scattered across the globe, each one with its own unique features and creatures. But they all have something in common—they need water. Rainforests are called "rain" forests for a reason. They receive an incredible amount of rainfall each year, sometimes as much as 260 inches! To put that into perspective, that's about 10 times more rain than many places in the United States get in a year. All that water helps create the lush, green environment that makes rainforests so special.

Rainforests also share another important quality: they're incredibly diverse. That means they have an enormous variety of plants, animals, and insects living together in one place. Scientists estimate that more than half of all the species on Earth live in rainforests, even though these forests cover less than 10% of the planet's surface. Imagine walking through a rainforest and discovering hundreds of different kinds of butterflies or dozens of types of frogs, all in one area. It's like a living library of life.

But these rainforests aren't just sitting there, separate from the rest of the world. They play a huge role in keeping our planet healthy. For example, the Amazon Rainforest is sometimes called the "lungs of the Earth" because it produces so much oxygen. It's also a giant sponge for carbon dioxide, a gas that contributes to climate change. By absorbing carbon dioxide and releasing oxygen, rainforests help regulate the air we all breathe, no matter where we live.

Rainforests are also connected to the water cycle. Trees and plants in the rainforest release moisture into the air, which eventually turns into clouds and rain. This doesn't just affect the rainforest itself—it impacts weather patterns all over the world. The Amazon, for instance, helps bring rain to places as far away as the United States. It's amazing to think that a tree in Brazil could play a role in creating a rainstorm thousands of miles away.

Despite their importance, rainforests are under threat. Many of them are being cut down to make room for farms, roads, and cities. This process, called deforestation, destroys habitats for animals and plants and disrupts the balance of the ecosystem. But people around the world are working to protect these incredible places. National parks, conservation projects, and even small actions like using less paper can help make a difference.

Why are rainforests important to the planet?

Rainforests act like Earth's air purifiers. Every single tree and plant in a rainforest absorbs carbon dioxide —a gas that can make the planet too warm—and replaces it with fresh oxygen. In fact, rainforests are responsible for producing about 20% of the oxygen we breathe. Without rainforests, the air we rely on would become harder to manage, and the balance of gases in the atmosphere would tilt in the wrong direction. It's like they're giant lungs for the Earth, quietly working day and night to keep everything in balance.

But their job doesn't stop with cleaning the air. Rainforests are also like Earth's water tanks. All those tall trees and lush plants soak up water from the ground and release it back into the air as moisture. That moisture eventually becomes clouds, and those clouds bring rain not just to the rainforest itself but to places far away. The Amazon, for instance, helps create rain that waters crops and fills rivers in countries thousands of miles away. Without rainforests, those clouds wouldn't form, and many parts of the world could experience droughts.

Beyond air and water, rainforests play a key role in protecting the soil. When rain pours down, the roots of rainforest trees act like anchors, holding the soil in place. Without these trees, heavy rains would wash the soil away, making it harder for new plants to grow. This process is called erosion, and it can turn a lush, green area into a barren, lifeless one. By keeping the soil healthy, rainforests ensure that plants, animals, and even people who depend on the land can survive.

Now, think about food. Have you ever eaten a banana, enjoyed a piece of chocolate, or tasted a juicy mango? All these foods—and many more—come from plants that grow in rainforests. Rainforests provide not just food but also spices like cinnamon and vanilla. These plants have been feeding people and animals for thousands of years. Imagine life without chocolate. It's hard to picture, isn't it?

But it's not just about what we eat. Rainforests are treasure chests of medicine. More than 25% of the medicines we use today come from plants found in rainforests. Scientists have discovered plants that help treat diseases like cancer, malaria, and heart conditions. And here's the exciting part: there are still thousands of rainforest plants that haven't been studied yet. Who knows what cures or treatments they might hold? Every time a part of the rainforest is destroyed, we lose the chance to discover something new that could save lives.

Rainforests are also home to more animals, plants, and insects than any other place on Earth. From the tiny dart frog to the enormous jaguar, rainforests are bursting with life. Each creature has a role to play. For example, bats help spread seeds by eating fruits and then dropping the seeds far away from the parent tree. Without bats, some rainforest trees wouldn't grow, and without those trees, animals that rely on them for food or shelter would struggle to survive. It's like a giant web where everything is connected, and if one part is lost, the whole web starts to unravel.

Even creatures you might not think about, like insects, are important. Take ants, for example. Some rainforest ants work together in armies, cleaning up dead plants and animals. Others help plants grow by spreading seeds or keeping harmful insects away. It might not sound glamorous, but without these tiny workers, the rainforest ecosystem would fall apart.

Rainforests also help regulate the planet's climate. When trees and plants absorb carbon dioxide, they help reduce the amount of heat-trapping gases in the atmosphere. This process slows down climate change and keeps the Earth from getting too hot. Rainforests are like a natural air-conditioning system for the planet, keeping everything cool and comfortable. Without them, temperatures could rise dramatically, leading to more extreme weather events like hurricanes, heatwaves, and floods.

And let's not forget the cultural importance of rainforests. For thousands of years, indigenous peoples have lived in harmony with these forests, relying on them for food, medicine, and shelter. Their knowledge of the rainforest is incredible—they know which plants can heal a wound, which fruits are safe to eat, and how to find water during a dry spell. Protecting rainforests isn't just about saving trees and animals; it's also about respecting and preserving the cultures and traditions of the people who call these forests home.

Rainforests also inspire us in ways that go beyond science or survival. They're places of wonder and beauty, filled with sounds, colors, and smells that can't be found anywhere else. Imagine standing in a rainforest and hearing the call of a toucan, smelling the sweet scent of blooming orchids, or feeling the cool mist from a nearby waterfall. Rainforests remind us of the incredible variety and creativity of life on Earth. They spark curiosity and a sense of adventure, making us want to learn more about the world we live in.

1

LAYERS OF THE RAINFOREST

Emergent Layer

The emergent layer is the very top of the rainforest, made up of trees that grow higher than the dense canopy below. These trees can reach heights of 200 feet or more, and their branches spread out wide, like enormous umbrellas. They're tough, too, able to withstand strong winds and heavy rains that sweep through the forest. While the layers below are shaded and damp, the emergent layer basks in sunlight, making it a hotspot for life that thrives in the open sky.

You might think being up so high would be lonely, but the emergent layer is anything but quiet. Birds with brightly colored feathers dart through the branches, calling to one another. Parrots squawk and chatter, their voices carrying across the treetops. Eagles and hawks soar overhead, scanning the ground below for food. It's a busy, bustling neighborhood— just one that happens to be hundreds of feet in the air.

One of the most famous residents of the emergent layer is the harpy eagle. This powerful bird is one of the largest eagles in the world, with wings that stretch nearly seven feet across. Harpy eagles hunt monkeys and sloths, swooping down from the treetops with incredible speed and precision. Despite their size, these eagles are masters of stealth, gliding silently through the air before striking. It's easy to see why they're considered the kings and queens of the emergent layer.

But it's not just birds that call this layer home. Monkeys are also frequent visitors, leaping from tree to tree with astonishing agility. Species like spider monkeys and howler monkeys spend much of their time up here, using their long tails as an extra hand to grip branches. Their acrobatics are both a way to travel and a way to stay safe—sticking to the treetops keeps them out of reach of ground-dwelling predators like jaguars.

Insects, too, have carved out a niche in the emergent layer. Some of the most dazzling butterflies in the rainforest flutter through the open sky, their wings catching the sunlight in flashes of blue, orange, and gold. Beetles and ants scuttle along branches, often going unnoticed but playing vital roles in the ecosystem. Even in the highest reaches of the forest, life finds a way to thrive.

The trees themselves are just as fascinating as the creatures they support. Many of the emergent trees are hardwood species like mahogany and kapok. The kapok tree, in particular, is one of the rainforest's most iconic giants. Its trunk is enormous—so wide that it would take several people holding hands to circle it—and its branches form a sprawling crown at the top. Kapok trees can live for hundreds of years, serving as a foundation for the rainforest's ecosystem. Birds, insects, and mammals all rely on these towering trees for shelter, food, and nesting sites.

To survive in such an exposed environment, the trees of the emergent layer have developed unique adaptations. Their roots, called buttress roots, spread wide and dig deep to anchor them firmly in the ground. This helps them stay upright, even during strong storms. The leaves at the tops of these trees are often smaller than those lower down, allowing them to handle the intense sunlight without losing too much water. It's a delicate balance, but these trees have mastered the art of thriving in one of the most challenging parts of the rainforest.

But why do these trees grow so tall in the first place? The answer lies in competition. In the rainforest, sunlight is a precious resource, and every plant is racing to reach it. By growing taller than their neighbors, the trees of the emergent layer gain an advantage. They soak up the sun's rays, converting that energy into food through photosynthesis. In turn, this energy flows through the entire ecosystem, feeding the plants, animals, and insects that depend on the rainforest for survival.

Up here, the view is breathtaking. If you could climb to the top of an emergent tree and look out, you'd see a sea of green stretching as far as the eye can see. The canopy below looks like a dense, endless carpet, with occasional bursts of color from flowering trees. The wind rushes through the branches, carrying the sounds of the rainforest—a symphony of chirps, calls, and rustling leaves. It's a perspective that few people ever get to experience, but one that reveals the incredible beauty and complexity of the rainforest.

The emergent layer isn't just a home for wildlife; it's also a vital part of the rainforest's role in the planet's health. By capturing sunlight and turning it into energy, these trees help regulate the Earth's climate. They absorb massive amounts of carbon dioxide, storing it in their trunks and releasing oxygen into the air. This process helps slow down climate change and keeps the atmosphere balanced. The trees of the emergent layer are like silent guardians, working tirelessly to keep our planet healthy.

Canopy

The canopy layer sits just below the emergent layer, but it's where most of the rainforest's action happens. About 80% of the rainforest's animals live here, making it the busiest and most crowded layer of all. Think of it as the heart of the rainforest—a level where plants and animals interact constantly, each one playing a role in the grand drama of the ecosystem.

Imagine standing on a platform high in the trees, looking out over the canopy. It would feel like stepping onto another planet. Leaves stretch in every direction, forming a patchwork of greens, yellows, and even hints of red or purple from flowering plants. Vines dangle and twist, like ropes on a giant playground. The air is thick with the sound of insects buzzing, birds calling, and the occasional rustle of something moving among the branches.

One of the canopy's most fascinating features is its sheer variety of plants. Trees in the canopy grow close together, their branches often intertwined. Epiphytes, or air plants, cling to the branches, taking in moisture and nutrients from the air rather than from the soil. Orchids and bromeliads are common epiphytes, their vibrant flowers adding splashes of color to the sea of green. Bromeliads are especially amazing—they can hold small pools of water in their leaves, creating tiny ecosystems where frogs, insects, and even small birds might live.

But the canopy isn't just a place for plants. It's also a superhighway for animals. Monkeys are some of the most skilled travelers here, leaping from branch to branch with incredible agility. Spider monkeys, for example, use their long, prehensile tails like extra hands, wrapping them around branches to swing gracefully through the trees. These tails are so strong that they can support the monkey's entire weight, leaving their hands free to grab food or defend themselves.

Birds are another dominant force in the canopy. Toucans, with their brightly colored beaks, hop from tree to tree, searching for fruits to eat. Their beaks may look heavy, but they're actually light and perfectly designed for reaching into narrow spaces to grab food. Parrots are also common in the canopy, their vivid feathers standing out against the green backdrop. These intelligent birds often travel in noisy flocks, their squawks and chatter filling the air.

Insects are everywhere in the canopy, and their diversity is staggering. Ants march in lines along branches, some species working together to build nests out of leaves. Butterflies and moths flit between flowers, sipping nectar and pollinating plants as they go. One of the most intriguing insects of the canopy is the leafcutter ant. These tiny creatures are incredibly strong for their size, cutting pieces of leaves and carrying them back to their nests. But they don't eat the leaves—they use them to grow a special type of fungus, which becomes their food.

Reptiles and amphibians also thrive in the canopy, often blending in so well with their surroundings that they're nearly invisible. Chameleons are masters of disguise, changing their skin color to match the leaves and branches around them. Tree frogs, with their sticky toe pads, cling effortlessly to the slick surfaces of leaves, sometimes hiding in bromeliads' water pools. Snakes, too, are part of this hidden world. The emerald tree boa, for instance, coils itself around branches, its green scales making it almost indistinguishable from the foliage.

Life in the canopy isn't just about survival—it's also about partnerships. Many plants and animals in this layer depend on each other in surprising ways. Take figs and fig wasps, for example. Fig trees produce fruit year-round, making them a reliable food source for many animals. But the tree has its own secret helper: the fig wasp. These tiny insects pollinate the figs, ensuring that new trees can grow. In return, the wasps lay their eggs inside the fruit, giving their larvae a safe place to develop. It's a perfect exchange that benefits both species.

The canopy also plays a critical role in the rainforest's larger ecosystem. It acts as a barrier, catching rain before it hits the ground and slowing its fall. This helps prevent soil erosion and ensures that the water is absorbed gradually, feeding the plants and trees below. The canopy also traps heat and moisture, creating the humid, warm conditions that rainforests are known for. Without the canopy, the rainforest would lose much of its unique character—and its ability to support such a wide range of life.

But the canopy isn't always a peaceful place. It's also a battleground. Predators like hawks and eagles patrol the skies above, swooping down to catch their prey. Smaller creatures have to stay alert, blending into the leaves or staying perfectly still to avoid being spotted. Competition for food is fierce, too. Fruits and seeds are a valuable resource, and animals like monkeys, birds, and squirrels often compete for the same meals.

Exploring the canopy feels like stepping into a bustling city, where every inch is occupied by something alive and active. But unlike a city, this layer is constantly changing. Leaves grow and fall, flowers bloom and wither, and animals move in and out, all part of the never-ending cycle of life. It's a dynamic, ever-shifting world that's both fragile and resilient, holding the rainforest together like a living, breathing network.

For scientists, the canopy is one of the most exciting—and challenging—places to study. Reaching it often requires climbing ropes, towering platforms, or even specially designed cranes. Once they're up there, researchers can uncover secrets about how the rainforest works, from the way plants and animals interact to how the canopy helps regulate the planet's climate. Each discovery brings us closer to understanding the incredible complexity of this layer and why it's so important to protect.

Understory

Step beneath the dense canopy of the rainforest, and you'll find yourself in a dim, shadowy realm known as the understory. Here, the sunlight that streams so brightly into the emergent layer and the canopy above barely trickles through. It's cooler and quieter, but far from empty. The understory is alive with plants and animals that have adapted to thrive in its shaded, humid environment. It's a world of mystery and stillness, where the more you look, the more you'll see.

The first thing you notice in the understory is the calm. The high energy of the canopy—where monkeys leap and parrots squawk—is replaced by a hushed atmosphere. The leaves overhead form a thick shield, letting through only tiny splashes of sunlight. The ground feels damp underfoot, and the air is heavy with moisture. This is where shadows dominate, and creatures blend into the surroundings, relying on camouflage to stay hidden from predators.

Plants in the understory are masters of survival. With so little light, they've developed clever ways to make the most of what they get. Their leaves are often much larger than those of canopy plants, like solar panels designed to capture every last bit of sunlight. Many understory plants grow slowly, conserving energy and waiting for a rare opportunity—perhaps a fallen branch or a dying tree—to create an opening in the canopy above. When that moment comes, these patient plants spring into action, growing quickly to take advantage of the new light.

You'll also find some of the rainforest's most unique and fascinating plants in the understory. Take orchids, for example. These delicate flowers often grow on tree trunks, adding splashes of color to the shadows. Some orchids are so perfectly camouflaged that they look like part of the tree bark, making them almost impossible to spot unless you're looking very closely. Other plants, like ferns and philodendrons, form lush carpets along the ground, their feathery leaves adding to the understory's dense, green texture.

But plants aren't the only ones playing hide-and-seek in this shadowy world. Animals in the understory have some of the most creative camouflage in the rainforest. Leaf-tailed geckos, for example, are so well-hidden that they look exactly like dried leaves, complete with veins and edges. They cling to branches, blending into the background so perfectly that even a sharp-eyed predator might miss them.

Another master of disguise is the stick insect. These insects have bodies shaped like twigs, allowing them to vanish into the branches and leaves they rest on. Some stick insects are so convincing that even their movements mimic the swaying of a twig in the breeze. It's not just about hiding—it's about becoming invisible in plain sight.

The understory is also home to one of the rainforest's most famous hunters: the jaguar. With its golden coat covered in black rosettes, the jaguar is built for stealth. It moves silently through the shadows, using the dim light to its advantage as it stalks its prey. Jaguars are incredibly strong, able to climb trees or drag heavy kills, and they're not picky eaters. From deer to capybaras to fish, these big cats can hunt a wide variety of animals. In the understory, where visibility is low, their patience and strength make them formidable predators.

While jaguars dominate the larger prey, smaller hunters like snakes also thrive in the understory. The emerald tree boa, with its brilliant green scales, coils itself around branches, waiting for an unsuspecting bird or mammal to wander close. Its ambush strategy is perfectly suited to the understory, where its camouflage and stillness allow it to go unnoticed until the last moment.

Insects and other small creatures are everywhere in the understory, and they play a critical role in keeping the ecosystem running smoothly. Ants, for instance, are some of the busiest workers here. Army ants form massive colonies that move across the forest floor in search of food, devouring everything in their path. Leafcutter ants march in long lines, carrying pieces of leaves back to their nests to grow their special fungus. These tiny workers may go unnoticed, but their activity is essential to the health of the rainforest.

Frogs are another common sight in the understory, particularly during the rainy season when the air is thick with their calls. The poison dart frog is one of the most striking residents of this layer. These tiny frogs, often no bigger than a thumbnail, have brightly colored skin that warns predators of their toxicity. Their vivid colors—ranging from bright blue to fiery orange—are like a neon sign that says, "Don't eat me!" Despite their small size, poison dart frogs are a powerful presence in the understory.

The understory's humidity creates the perfect conditions for fungi, which grow in a variety of shapes, sizes, and colors. Some fungi glow faintly in the dark, lighting up the forest floor with an eerie greenish hue. These bioluminescent fungi, sometimes called "ghost mushrooms," feed on decaying plant material, breaking it down into nutrients that enrich the soil. Their role is crucial in the cycle of life and death that sustains the rainforest.

But the understory isn't all stillness and quiet. During the rainy season, it comes alive with activity. Rivers and streams swell, and the sound of rushing water echoes through the trees. Insects buzz, frogs croak, and birds with haunting calls add their voices to the mix. It's a reminder that even in the shadows, the rainforest is teeming with life.

For the indigenous peoples who have lived in rainforests for generations, the understory is a place of knowledge and resources. Many plants found here have medicinal properties, used to treat everything from cuts and bruises to fevers and infections. The understory is also a source of food, with fruits, nuts, and small animals providing sustenance. Learning to navigate this shadowy layer requires deep understanding and respect for the forest.

Forest Floor

The forest floor is where the rainforest begins and ends. Leaves, branches, and fruits fall from the trees above, creating a thick carpet of organic material. Over time, this layer of debris is broken down by decomposers like fungi, bacteria, and insects. These tiny workers are some of the most important members of the rainforest, turning dead plants and animals into nutrients that feed the soil and support new growth. It's a recycling system so efficient that hardly anything goes to waste.

ONE OF THE most fascinating decomposers on the forest floor is the mushroom. Fungi come in all shapes and sizes here, from tiny button-like forms to large, shelf-like structures growing on fallen logs. Some fungi glow faintly in the dark, a phenomenon called bioluminescence. These "glowing mushrooms" light up the forest floor with an eerie greenish hue, like nature's version of a nightlight. But fungi don't just look cool—they're essential to the rainforest's health. They break down dead wood and leaves, releasing nutrients back into the soil and creating a foundation for life above.

WHILE FUNGI WORK on plant material, other decomposers handle the animal side of things. Beetles, ants, and worms crawl through the leaf litter, cleaning up dead insects and animals. One of the most efficient clean-up crews is made up of dung beetles. These industrious insects roll animal droppings into neat little balls, which they bury and use as a food source. It might sound gross, but dung beetles play a critical role in keeping the forest floor clean and fertile.

AMID THE DECOMPOSERS, larger creatures make their homes in the shadows. The forest floor is a refuge for secretive animals that prefer to stay hidden. Jaguars, for example, move silently through the undergrowth, their golden coats blending perfectly with the dappled light and shadow. These powerful cats are solitary hunters, stalking prey like deer and wild pigs with incredible patience. Jaguars are so stealthy that you'd rarely see one, even if it were nearby.

OTHER PREDATORS, like snakes, also thrive on the forest floor. The green anaconda, one of the largest snakes in the world, slithers through rivers and swamps, waiting to ambush its prey. Despite its size, the anaconda is a master of camouflage, its patterned skin blending with the murky water and tangled roots. Smaller snakes, like the eyelash viper, use their bright colors to warn predators that they're dangerous. These snakes often coil themselves near the ground, hidden among fallen leaves or low-hanging branches.

· · ·

IN THE STILLNESS of the forest floor, you'll also find creatures that move so quietly they're almost invisible. Tapirs, which look like a mix between a pig and a small elephant, wander through the undergrowth in search of fruits and leaves. With their short trunks, they can grab food from the ground or low-hanging plants. Tapirs are shy and often nocturnal, using the cover of darkness to avoid predators. Despite their size, they're surprisingly agile, able to navigate the dense forest with ease.

ONE OF THE forest floor's most unusual residents is the giant anteater. With its long snout and sticky tongue, it's perfectly designed to eat ants and termites, which it finds by tearing open nests with its sharp claws. Watching a giant anteater at work is mesmerizing—it moves slowly and deliberately, using its keen sense of smell to locate its next meal. Despite their calm appearance, anteaters are strong and can defend themselves fiercely if threatened.

THE FOREST FLOOR isn't just home to animals; it's also a crucial layer for plants. Seedlings sprout in the nutri-ent-rich soil, waiting for their chance to grow. Some seeds can lie dormant for years, biding their time until a gap in the canopy above lets in enough light for them to thrive. This patience pays off when a tree falls, creating an opening that allows sunlight to reach the forest floor. In these rare moments, the competition among seedlings is fierce, with the fastest-growing plants taking the lead.

BUT LIFE on the forest floor isn't easy. The lack of sunlight makes it a challenging environment for plants and animals alike. Many creatures have developed unique adaptations to survive here. Frogs, for instance, often have brightly colored skin that warns predators of their toxicity. Others, like the glass frog, are almost completely transparent, making them nearly invisible against the wet leaves and rocks.

INSECTS, too, have found ways to thrive in this dark, humid world. Army ants march in massive columns, hunting anything in their path. These ants work together with incredible precision, forming bridges with their own bodies to cross gaps and reach their prey. Leafcutter ants, meanwhile, carry pieces of leaves back to their underground nests, where they use them to grow fungus for food. It's like a tiny, bustling city hidden beneath the soil.

· · ·

THE FOREST FLOOR also plays a critical role in the rainforest's water cycle. When rain falls, the thick layer of leaves and soil absorbs the water, preventing it from washing away. This slow absorption process helps recharge underground water sources and feeds the roots of the towering trees above. Without the forest floor, the rainforest's entire ecosystem would struggle to survive.

2

PLANTS OF THE RAINFOREST

Walking through a rainforest feels like stepping into a giant green kingdom, where plants rule everything. Everywhere you look, there are plants—on the ground, climbing up trees, hanging in the air. But some plants stand out more than others, not just for how they look but for the incredible ways they've adapted to survive in this lush and competitive world. Orchids, bromeliads, and kapok trees are three of the most fascinating plants in the rainforest, each playing a unique role in this vibrant ecosystem.

Let's start with orchids. These flowers aren't just pretty—they're some of the most clever and diverse plants on the planet. There are thousands of orchid species in rainforests, and they come in almost every color and shape you can imagine. Some are small and delicate, while others have blooms as big as your hand. But what really sets orchids apart is their ability to grow almost anywhere. They don't need soil like most plants. Instead, many orchids are epiphytes, which means they grow on other plants, like tree trunks and branches.

Orchids use their roots to cling to trees, where they can soak up moisture from the humid air and nutrients from decaying leaves and debris. This clever adaptation allows them to avoid the crowded forest floor, where sunlight is scarce and competition is fierce. From their high perch in the canopy or understory, orchids can get just enough light to thrive. Some orchids even have special relationships with insects, using their colorful petals and sweet scents to attract pollinators. A bee or butterfly lands on the flower, collects pollen, and carries it to another orchid, helping the plant reproduce. It's a perfect partnership that benefits both the orchid and the insect.

But not all orchids play fair. Some are sneaky, mimicking the appearance of other flowers to trick insects into visiting them. These orchids don't offer nectar as a reward, but by the time the insect realizes it's been duped, it's already carrying the orchid's pollen to another flower. This kind of trickery shows just how resourceful and adaptable orchids can be in the rainforest.

While orchids are masters of elegance, bromeliads

bring a splash of color and practicality to the rainforest. These plants are often shaped like funnels or cups, and they're experts at collecting water. Bromeliads use their tightly packed leaves to trap rainwater, creating tiny reservoirs that can hold gallons of water. These reservoirs become miniature ecosystems, home to frogs, insects, and even small fish. Some bromeliads are so large that entire families of creatures can live inside them, using the water for drinking and laying eggs.

Like orchids, many bromeliads are epiphytes, growing high in the trees. But their water-collecting ability means they're not entirely dependent on rain. They can survive in dry spells by using the water stored in their leaves. This adaptation makes bromeliads incredibly resilient, able to thrive in a variety of conditions within the rainforest. Their bright, often neon-colored flowers add to their appeal, attracting pollinators like hummingbirds and bees.

One of the most famous bromeliads is the pineapple plant. Yes, the same fruit you find in the grocery store originally came from bromeliads in tropical rainforests. While wild pineapple plants are smaller than the ones we eat today, they're a reminder of how rainforests contribute to the foods we enjoy every day.

And then there are the kapok trees, the towering giants of the rainforest. Kapok trees can grow over 200 feet tall, with trunks so wide that it might take ten people holding hands to wrap around one. These massive trees dominate the emergent layer, rising above the canopy like skyscrapers. Their branches form a sprawling network that provides shelter for countless animals, from monkeys and birds to ants and lizards.

The kapok tree is a lifeline for many species in the rainforest. Its branches are often covered in epiphytes, including orchids and bromeliads, which use the tree as a platform to reach sunlight. Birds build nests in its branches, while bats roost in its hollow trunk. Even the tree's fruit, which contains cotton-like fibers, provides food for animals and helps disperse seeds throughout the forest.

Kapok trees are also important to people. Indigenous communities in the rainforest have used the kapok tree for generations, relying on it for food, medicine, and materials. The cotton-like fibers inside the tree's fruit are used to make pillows, mattresses, and even life vests. The bark, leaves, and seeds are believed to have medicinal properties, treating everything from fevers to wounds. For these communities, the kapok tree is more than just a plant—it's a symbol of life and sustainability.

Despite their strength and size, kapok trees face challenges. Their wood is lightweight and easy to cut, making them a target for logging. When kapok trees are removed from the rainforest, it's not just the tree that's lost. The animals and plants that depend on it are left without a home, disrupting the delicate balance of the ecosystem. Protecting these giants is essential for preserving the rainforest as a whole.

Carnivorous plants and their unusual diets

Tucked away in the shadowy corners of the rainforest, where the soil is often wet and lacking in nutrients, some plants have developed an astonishing strategy to survive. These are the carnivorous plants, hunters of the plant world, that get their nutrition not from the soil but from creatures that crawl, fly, or stumble into their traps. It's a fascinating twist on what we usually think plants do—they don't just sit still and soak up sunlight; they actively catch and digest their food.

The idea of a plant eating animals might sound like something out of a spooky story, but in the rainforest, it's a clever adaptation. The soil in many parts of the rainforest can be surprisingly poor in nutrients. With so much competition among plants, some species have evolved to get their nutrients from a different source: the insects and small animals around them. This unusual diet has led to some of the most creative and bizarre strategies in the plant kingdom.

One of the most famous carnivorous plants is the pitcher plant. It doesn't look like a traditional plant with leaves and flowers. Instead, it has long, tube-like structures called pitchers that act as traps. These pitchers are brightly colored and often have sweet-smelling nectar around the rim to lure insects. When an unsuspecting insect lands on the pitcher, it finds the surface slippery and falls inside. The inside of the pitcher is lined with tiny, downward-pointing hairs that make climbing back out nearly impossible. At the bottom of the pitcher is a pool of digestive enzymes—essentially the plant's stomach—that breaks down the insect into nutrients the plant can absorb.

Pitcher plants come in all shapes and sizes, and some are large enough to trap creatures as big as frogs or even small rodents. Imagine a mouse crawling onto a pitcher plant, only to slide down into the waiting pool at the bottom. While this might sound gruesome, it's an incredibly effective way for the plant to survive in an environment where nutrients are hard to come by. And because pitcher plants come in so many sizes, they've adapted to catch a wide range of prey, from tiny ants to much larger animals.

Another remarkable carnivorous plant is the sundew. Sundews are small and delicate-looking, with leaves covered in sticky, glistening droplets that look like morning dew—hence their name. But these "dew-drops" are actually sticky traps. When an insect lands on a sundew's leaf, it gets stuck in the sticky substance. As the insect struggles to escape, the plant's tentacle-like hairs slowly curl around it, holding it tightly. Once the insect is trapped, the sundew releases digestive enzymes to break down the insect's body and absorb its nutrients.

Watching a sundew catch its prey is like seeing a slow-motion drama unfold. The plant's movements are almost imperceptible, but they're precise and deliberate. Sundews may be small, but their strategy is incredibly effective, and they're found in rainforests around the world.

If you think sundews are impressive, wait until you hear about the Venus flytrap. While not exclusively a rainforest plant, it's often included in the same family of fascinating carnivorous plants. The Venus flytrap has jaw-like leaves with sensitive hairs on the inside. When an insect brushes against these hairs twice in quick succession, the "jaws" snap shut in less than a second. The trapped insect is then digested over several days. The speed and precision of a Venus flytrap's snap make it one of the most iconic and dramatic carnivorous plants.

In tropical rainforests, another standout predator is the bladderwort. Unlike pitcher plants or sundews, bladderworts live in water, and their traps are even harder to see. These plants have tiny, bladder-like structures that act as underwater vacuums. When a small aquatic creature, like a water flea, swims too close, the bladder snaps open, sucking the creature inside in a fraction of a second. Once inside, the animal is digested, and the bladder resets, ready to catch the next victim. Bladderworts might be small, but they're some of the fastest and most efficient hunters in the plant world.

Each of these carnivorous plants has evolved to thrive in specific niches within the rainforest. Pitcher plants often grow in swampy or low-lying areas where the soil is waterlogged and lacks nutrients. Sundews can be found in sandy or acidic soils, while bladderworts dominate the small pools and streams scattered throughout the forest. Their ability to catch and digest prey gives them a huge advantage in environments where other plants struggle to survive.

But carnivorous plants aren't just interesting for their diets—they also play important roles in the rainforest ecosystem. By catching and eating insects, they help control populations of certain species, keeping the balance of the ecosystem in check. At the same time, their flowers provide nectar for pollinators like bees and butterflies, just like non-carnivorous plants. This dual role as both predator and provider makes them unique contributors to the rainforest's delicate web of life.

Carnivorous plants are also a reminder of how adaptable nature can be. These plants have found a way to turn a challenging environment into an opportunity, using their unusual strategies to outcompete other plants. Their creativity and resourcefulness are a testament to the incredible diversity of life in the rainforest.

For scientists, carnivorous plants are endlessly fascinating. They offer clues about how plants can evolve in response to their environments, and studying them can even lead to discoveries in other fields, like medicine and engineering. For example, the slippery surface of a pitcher plant has inspired designs for non-stick coatings and other technologies. It's amazing to think that a plant growing quietly in the rainforest could have such an impact on human innovation.

Adaptations for survival

One of the most striking adaptations you'll notice in rainforest plants is their leaves. They're often large, glossy, and dotted with distinctive features that make them stand out. But these aren't just for show—each unique trait plays a critical role in helping the plant survive.

Take a closer look at the leaves of many rainforest plants, and you'll notice something called drip tips. These are pointed ends on leaves that help rainwater roll off quickly. In the rainforest, where it rains almost daily, plants are constantly drenched. If water collects and sits on a leaf for too long, it can cause fungi and bacteria to grow, damaging the plant. Drip tips act like tiny rain gutters, allowing water to slide off smoothly and keeping the leaves healthy. It's a small detail that makes a big difference.

The size of leaves is another fascinating adaptation. In the shady understory of the rainforest, sunlight barely reaches the ground. Plants here have evolved to grow large leaves, almost like solar panels, to capture as much light as possible. These oversized leaves often have deep green colors, packed with chlorophyll to maximize photosynthesis. For plants in this dimly lit environment, every ray of sunlight is precious.

But not all large leaves are found in the understory. In swampy areas of the rainforest, you might see giant water lilies with leaves so big they could hold a small child. These massive leaves float on the surface of water, supported by a network of veins that keep them strong. The wide surface area allows the plant to soak up sunlight while also providing a safe resting place for frogs, insects, and even birds. It's a perfect example of a plant adapting not just to survive but to thrive in its unique environment.

Rainforest plants have also developed ways to climb toward the light, escaping the darkness of the forest floor. Lianas, or woody vines, are experts at this. They start their lives on the ground but quickly latch onto nearby trees, winding their way upward. By using trees as support, lianas save energy they would otherwise need to build thick trunks. This strategy allows them to reach the canopy and bask in the sunlight without competing directly with towering trees.

Another group of plants, called epiphytes, skips the forest floor entirely. Instead of growing in soil, they attach themselves to the branches and trunks of trees. Orchids and bromeliads are two well-known examples. By living high up in the canopy, these plants avoid the crowded ground and get direct access to sunlight. But living in the trees comes with challenges —there's no soil to hold water or nutrients. Epiphytes have adapted by developing special roots and leaves that can absorb moisture and nutrients from the air and rain. It's a brilliant way to make the most of a tough situation.

Rainforest plants have also mastered the art of self-defense. With so many animals around, plants are constantly at risk of being eaten. To protect themselves, many have evolved physical and chemical defenses. Some plants grow sharp thorns or spines to keep hungry animals at bay. Others produce toxic chemicals in their leaves, making them taste bitter or even poisonous. For example, the leaves of the rubber tree contain latex, a sticky substance that deters insects and other pests.

In some cases, plants form alliances with animals to protect themselves. The acacia tree is a great example. It provides shelter and food for ants in its hollow thorns. In return, the ants patrol the tree, attacking any animals or other plants that threaten it. This partnership benefits both the tree and the ants, showing how even in the competitive rainforest, cooperation can be a survival strategy.

Water is both a blessing and a challenge in the rainforest. While there's plenty of rain, it doesn't always soak into the soil evenly. Some areas are waterlogged, while others dry out quickly. To deal with this, many rainforest plants have developed specialized root systems. Mangroves, for instance, grow in salty, swampy areas and have roots that rise above the water like stilts. These aerial roots help the tree breathe and stay stable in shifting mud. Meanwhile, other trees grow buttress roots—massive, flared structures at the base of the trunk that provide support and help the tree absorb nutrients from the shallow soil.

Even seeds in the rainforest have unique adaptations. Some are lightweight and equipped with wings or fluff, allowing them to be carried by the wind to new locations. Others rely on animals to spread them. Brightly colored fruits attract birds, monkeys, and other animals, which eat the fruit and carry the seeds to different parts of the forest. Some seeds are even designed to survive being eaten, passing through an animal's digestive system unharmed before being deposited in a new spot.

How plants support the ecosystem

Rainforest plants are like the ultimate multitaskers. They produce oxygen, filter water, provide food, and even build homes for other creatures. Everything starts with photosynthesis—the magical process that allows plants to convert sunlight into energy. During photosynthesis, plants take in carbon dioxide and release oxygen, creating the air we breathe. The sheer number of plants in the rainforest means they pump out enormous amounts of oxygen, earning the rainforest its nickname: "the lungs of the Earth."

But plants don't just help us; they're vital for all life in the rainforest. Trees in the emergent layer and canopy act as giant umbrellas, shielding the forest floor from heavy rain and harsh sunlight. Their leaves and branches catch raindrops, slowing their fall and preventing soil erosion. Without these trees, rain would wash away the nutrient-rich topsoil, making it nearly impossible for other plants to grow.

Beyond their protective canopy, trees play another important role: they store water. Rainforest trees absorb massive amounts of rain through their roots and release it into the air as moisture. This process, called transpiration, helps create the rainforest's humid climate and fuels the water cycle. Moisture released by plants forms clouds that bring rain not only to the rainforest but also to regions far away. It's like the trees are working together to keep the planet hydrated.

Many rainforest plants also act as food factories. Their leaves, fruits, and seeds provide meals for countless animals, from tiny insects to enormous mammals. For example, fig trees produce fruit year-round, making them a reliable food source for birds, monkeys, bats, and even insects. In turn, these animals spread the tree's seeds, ensuring the next generation of fig trees can grow. It's a perfect partnership that benefits both the plants and the animals.

Other plants, like cacao trees, are the source of foods humans enjoy, such as chocolate. But in the rainforest, their fruits feed creatures like squirrels, toucans, and capuchin monkeys. These animals often act as seed dispersers, carrying the seeds far from the parent tree and giving them a better chance to germinate. The rainforest is full of these partnerships, where plants and animals work together in surprising ways.

Some plants go even further, providing not just food but also shelter. Bromeliads, with their water-holding leaves, are like tiny ponds high in the canopy. Frogs, insects, and even small birds use them as homes, raising their young in the water-filled leaves. Orchids often host ants that protect them from herbivores, while large trees like the kapok provide nesting sites for eagles, bats, and other animals.

Even decomposing plants play a critical role in the ecosystem. When leaves, fruits, and branches fall to the forest floor, they become food for decomposers like fungi, bacteria, and insects. These decomposers break down the plant material into nutrients, which enrich the soil and feed the next generation of plants. It's a continuous cycle of life and death, where nothing goes to waste.

Rainforest plants also support some of the tiniest but most important creatures in the ecosystem: pollinators. Flowers in the rainforest have evolved bright colors, unique shapes, and enticing scents to attract bees, butterflies, hummingbirds, and bats. These pollinators transfer pollen from one flower to another, allowing plants to produce seeds and fruits. Without this crucial service, many plants wouldn't be able to reproduce, and the entire ecosystem would suffer.

Some plants even play a role in controlling the weather. By releasing water vapor and influencing air currents, rainforest plants help regulate the temperature and precipitation patterns of the entire region. This isn't just important for the rainforest itself—it affects weather systems across the globe, showing how interconnected everything on Earth really is.

But perhaps the most astonishing way plants support the rainforest ecosystem is through their ability to form partnerships with other organisms. The acacia tree, for example, has a unique relationship with ants. The tree provides shelter and food for the ants in the form of hollow thorns and sweet nectar. In return, the ants protect the tree by attacking herbivores and even trimming away competing plants. This mutualistic relationship benefits both the tree and the ants, demonstrating the incredible teamwork found in the rainforest.

Another example is the role of rainforest plants in human life. Indigenous communities have relied on rainforest plants for thousands of years, using them for food, medicine, and materials. Plants like the rubber tree provide latex for making rubber, while others, like the cinchona tree, produce quinine, a medicine used to treat malaria. Even today, scientists continue to study rainforest plants for potential cures to diseases and other valuable resources.

3

ANIMALS OF THE RAINFOREST

The rainforest hums with life. Every rustle of a leaf, every chirp, croak, or screech is a sign that the animals here are busy living out their stories. It's a place where jaguars silently stalk through the shadows, sloths move so slowly they seem part of the trees, toucans flash like flying rainbows, and frogs with skin that could rival a box of crayons leap from leaf to leaf. Each creature in this wild and colorful world plays a role in the grand puzzle of the rainforest, adding its unique touch to the symphony of life.

Let's start with the jaguar, the king of the rainforest. With its golden coat marked by black rosettes, the jaguar blends perfectly into the dappled light of the forest floor. This big cat is a master hunter, known for its strength and stealth. Unlike most cats, jaguars are excellent swimmers and often hunt near rivers, feasting on fish, caimans, and even turtles. Their powerful jaws can crush the shells of turtles with ease, a skill that sets them apart from other predators. But jaguars aren't just hunters—they're also key to keeping the ecosystem balanced. By preying on herbivores, they prevent overgrazing and help maintain the delicate harmony of the forest.

High above the jaguar's domain, in the canopy, lives one of the rainforest's most iconic residents: the sloth. With their slow, deliberate movements and ever-present sleepy expressions, sloths seem like they have all the time in the world. Their unhurried pace helps them conserve energy and avoid detection by predators. Covered in coarse, greenish fur, sloths often look like part of the tree they're clinging to—a clever camouflage that keeps them safe. Their fur even hosts tiny ecosystems of its own, with algae, moths, and other microorganisms living among the hairs.

Sloths spend most of their lives hanging upside down, eating leaves, and sleeping. But every so often, they descend to the forest floor, moving clumsily on land compared to their graceful tree-climbing. Despite their sluggish reputation, sloths play an important role in the rainforest. By eating leaves and defecating in different locations, they help spread seeds, encouraging new plants to grow.

If sloths are the calm, quiet residents of the rainforest, toucans are its bold, noisy neighbors. With their oversized, brightly colored beaks, toucans are hard to miss. These birds use their impressive beaks to pluck fruit from trees, tossing it back with a quick flip of their heads. But toucans don't just eat fruit—they're also opportunistic feeders, occasionally snacking on insects, eggs, or even small reptiles.

Toucans are loud and social, often traveling in small groups and communicating with squawking calls that echo through the canopy. Their role in the rainforest goes beyond their striking appearance and chatter. By eating fruit and spreading seeds through their droppings, toucans help plants grow and thrive, ensuring the rainforest remains lush and vibrant.

Meanwhile, down in the damp understory, a tiny but mighty creature hops among the leaves: the poison dart frog. These frogs are some of the most colorful animals in the rainforest, with skin that ranges from bright blue to vivid orange to shiny green. Their dazzling colors aren't just for show—they serve as a warning to predators that these frogs are highly toxic. Indigenous people have used the poison from these frogs to coat the tips of blow darts, giving the frogs their name.

Despite their small size, poison dart frogs play a big role in the ecosystem. They help control insect populations, keeping pests in check. And like sloths and toucans, they contribute to seed dispersal by eating small fruits and passing the seeds through their digestive systems. Watching a poison dart frog hop across the forest floor is like seeing a tiny, living jewel in motion—a reminder of how even the smallest creatures can shine in the rainforest.

Not far from the poison dart frogs, another amphibian adds its voice to the rainforest chorus: the red-eyed tree frog. These frogs are masters of surprise, with bright red eyes and blue-striped sides that flash when they leap. During the day, they hide among leaves, blending in with their green surroundings. But at night, they come alive, hunting insects with their sticky tongues and navigating the trees with their suction-cup toes. Their ability to adapt to both the ground and the trees makes them versatile survivors in the complex rainforest ecosystem.

And then there are the reptiles. The rainforest is home to some of the most fascinating and fearsome reptiles on the planet. The emerald tree boa coils itself around branches, its green scales blending seamlessly with the foliage. This snake is a master of ambush, waiting patiently for prey to wander within striking distance. Unlike the jaguar, the boa doesn't rely on brute strength but instead uses its speed and constricting power to catch its meals.

Down by the rivers, caimans patrol the water's edge. These relatives of alligators are stealthy predators, snapping up fish, birds, and even mammals that come too close. With their armored bodies and sharp teeth, caimans might seem like the ultimate hunters. But like the jaguar, they play a role in keeping the ecosystem balanced, preventing any one species from dominating.

The rainforest wouldn't be complete without its winged inhabitants. From the canopy to the forest floor, birds fill the air with their songs and colors. Parrots, like the scarlet macaw, are particularly striking, with their bright red, blue, and yellow feathers. These intelligent birds are skilled problem solvers, using their strong beaks to crack open nuts and seeds. Parrots are also excellent mimics, capable of imitating the sounds of other animals and even human voices.

Insects and Microorganisms

Walk through a rainforest and you're likely to see lines of leafcutter ants marching diligently along trails they've carved into the ground. Each ant carries a piece of a leaf much larger than itself, like a tiny worker hauling a giant green sail. But the leaf isn't food for the ants—not directly, at least. Instead, the ants bring the leaves back to their underground nests, where they use them to grow a special kind of fungus. This fungus is what the ants eat, making them not just workers but also farmers. Their teamwork is incredible to watch, with each ant knowing exactly what role to play to keep the colony thriving.

Leafcutter ants are just one type of ant in the rainforest. Army ants are another, and they're like the special forces of the insect world. These ants don't build permanent nests; instead, they're always on the move, traveling in massive swarms that can include hundreds of thousands of individuals. As they march through the forest, they devour anything in their path —worms, spiders, even small lizards. Other animals, like birds, often follow army ants to snatch up the creatures fleeing from their advance. It's a vivid reminder of how interconnected life in the rainforest is, with one creature's actions rippling out to affect countless others.

While ants are the workhorses of the rainforest, butterflies are its artists. Their wings, painted with brilliant colors and intricate patterns, brighten the forest and attract pollinators to plants. Butterflies play a crucial role in helping plants reproduce. As they sip nectar from flowers, they pick up pollen on their legs and wings, carrying it to other flowers and allowing seeds to form. Some butterflies, like the blue morpho, are so striking that they seem like living jewels flitting through the canopy.

But butterflies don't start life as the graceful creatures we see. They begin as caterpillars, which munch their way through leaves, growing and shedding their skin several times before forming a chrysalis. Inside this protective shell, the caterpillar transforms into a butterfly, a process as magical as the rainforest itself. Caterpillars may seem like simple leaf-eaters, but their voracious appetites play a part in the ecosystem too, thinning out vegetation and helping maintain balance among the plants.

Not all insects are as flashy as butterflies. Many go unnoticed, working quietly in the background. Beetles, for instance, are among the rainforest's most diverse creatures. From shiny metallic beetles that glisten in the sunlight to camouflaged ones that blend into bark, these insects fill countless niches. Some beetles help decompose dead plants and animals, breaking them down into nutrients that enrich the soil. Others feed on fungi or scavenge for leftovers, playing their part in keeping the forest clean and fertile.

Decomposers, in fact, are some of the most important residents of the rainforest, even if they're often overlooked. These include not just beetles but also microorganisms like fungi and bacteria. When a tree falls or a plant dies, it's the decomposers that get to work, breaking down the organic matter into its basic building blocks. Without them, the rainforest would quickly become buried under a layer of leaves and debris, and the nutrients locked inside dead plants and animals would never return to the soil.

Fungi are particularly fascinating decomposers. Some fungi form delicate, umbrella-like mushrooms that pop up after a rainstorm, while others grow as thin, thread-like networks called mycelium, which spread underground or inside rotting wood. These mycelium networks are like the rainforest's recycling centers, breaking down tough materials like lignin and cellulose into nutrients that plants can absorb. Some fungi even form partnerships with trees, attaching to their roots and helping them absorb water and minerals in exchange for sugar. It's a relationship that benefits both the fungi and the trees, another example of the rainforest's intricate web of connections.

And then there are the smallest decomposers of all: bacteria. These microscopic organisms work silently but tirelessly, breaking down organic matter at a molecular level. They're so small that you'd need a powerful microscope to see them, but their impact is enormous. By turning dead plants and animals into nutrients, bacteria help fuel the growth of new life, ensuring that the rainforest continues to thrive.

Predator-prey relationships and food chains

Imagine a butterfly flitting gracefully from flower to flower, sipping nectar. To us, it seems carefree, but to a hunting mantis hiding nearby, that butterfly is dinner. Praying mantises are expert ambush hunters. With their long, spiky forelegs folded as if in prayer, they wait patiently for an insect to come close. Then, in a lightning-fast strike, they grab their prey. Their speed and precision are impressive, and it's easy to see why they've earned their reputation as fierce hunters.

But the butterfly isn't completely defenseless. Some butterflies, like the blue morpho, use their dazzling colors to confuse predators. When they open their wings, the vibrant blue flashes brightly, making it hard for a mantis—or any other predator—to focus on them. Other butterflies rely on mimicry, with wing patterns that resemble the eyes of a much larger animal, like an owl. This trick can scare off predators and give the butterfly a chance to escape.

Meanwhile, on the forest floor, another predator-prey drama is unfolding. Ants are some of the most abundant insects in the rainforest, and they're both hunters and prey. Army ants, for instance, move in massive swarms, hunting anything in their path. They'll take down insects, spiders, and even small lizards, leaving almost nothing behind. But army ants themselves are prey for other animals, like antbirds, which follow the swarms and snatch up the creatures trying to escape.

Among the ants' prey are termites, which have their own strategies for survival. Termites live in large colonies protected by soldiers with powerful jaws or chemical defenses. If a predator, like an anteater or an aardvark, attacks their mound, the termites fight back with surprising determination. But if the predator breaks through, it's a feast—anteaters, for instance, can eat thousands of termites in a single sitting, using their long, sticky tongues to scoop them up.

Higher up in the rainforest's layers, food chains grow even more intricate. Birds like toucans and parrots eat fruit and seeds, but they're also prey for larger birds of prey, like hawks and eagles. These predators have keen eyesight, allowing them to spot their next meal from far away. When a hawk swoops down on a parrot, it's a dramatic moment of speed and skill, showcasing the constant battle for survival in the rainforest.

Even tiny insects play vital roles in these food chains. Consider the role of pollinators like bees and butterflies. While they're busy gathering nectar from flowers, they're also spreading pollen, helping plants reproduce and create fruit. This fruit then becomes food for monkeys, birds, and other animals, linking insects to larger creatures in a web of connections.

In the darker, damper parts of the rainforest, the relationships between predators and prey take on an eerie quality. Take the case of assassin bugs, which use stealth and trickery to catch their prey. These insects inject venom into their victims, liquefying their insides before sucking them out. It's a gruesome but effective strategy, showing just how many creative ways predators in the rainforest have adapted to find food.

While insects are often prey for larger animals, they can also be the hunters. Giant centipedes, for instance, are fearsome predators in the rainforest. These long, multi-legged creatures can take down animals much larger than themselves, including small birds, frogs, and even bats. They use their sharp claws to inject venom into their prey, paralyzing it before feasting. It's a reminder that in the rainforest, size isn't always an advantage—sometimes, speed and venom are all you need.

But what about the tiniest players in the food chain? Microorganisms, like fungi and bacteria, might not seem like predators, but they're essential to the ecosystem. When a plant or animal dies, decomposers break it down into nutrients that feed the soil. Without them, the rainforest would become buried under layers of dead matter, and the food chains above would collapse. Fungi, in particular, play fascinating roles in these cycles. Some fungi even prey on living insects, trapping them with sticky threads or infecting them with spores that turn them into food for the fungi's growth.

Predator-prey relationships in the rainforest often involve clever strategies and surprising teamwork. For example, some plants rely on carnivorous insects to protect them from herbivores. Acacia trees, for instance, house ants in their hollow thorns, feeding them with nectar. In return, the ants attack any animal that tries to eat the tree's leaves. It's a win-win partnership that shows how even plants can participate in the rainforest's predator-prey dynamics.

4

THE RAINFOREST CLIMATE

Rainforests get their name for a reason—they're the wettest places on Earth. On average, tropical rainforests receive between 80 and 400 inches of rain every year. To put that into perspective, imagine the rainiest day you've ever experienced and multiply it by many, many more rainy days. In some rainforests, it rains almost every single day, and the storms can be spectacular, with thunder rumbling across the treetops and sheets of water pouring down like a curtain.

But the rain isn't just about getting everything wet. It's a crucial part of what makes the rainforest such a vibrant and lush environment. Plants need water to grow, and in the rainforest, there's no shortage of it. The constant rainfall ensures that even the tallest trees and the smallest mosses have enough moisture to thrive. Streams, rivers, and ponds crisscross the forest floor, providing water for animals and carrying nutrients throughout the ecosystem.

The rain doesn't just fall randomly—it's part of a bigger cycle that the rainforest helps create. Trees and plants in the rainforest release water vapor into the air through a process called transpiration. This water vapor rises into the atmosphere, forming clouds. When the clouds become heavy with moisture, the water falls back to the Earth as rain, starting the cycle all over again. The rainforest is like a self-sustaining water factory, creating its own weather and keeping the ecosystem in balance.

Humidity is another defining feature of the rainforest climate. The air is almost always saturated with moisture, with humidity levels often reaching 80% or higher. This high humidity gives the rainforest its steamy, almost magical atmosphere. You can see it in the mist that hangs between the trees and feel it in the warm, sticky air that clings to your skin. It's like the rainforest is constantly wrapped in a blanket of moisture.

This humidity creates the perfect conditions for life to flourish. Many plants and animals in the rainforest depend on the damp air to survive. Orchids and bromeliads, for example, absorb water directly from the air, while frogs rely on the humidity to keep their skin moist. Even microorganisms, like fungi and bacteria, thrive in the damp environment, breaking down organic material and recycling nutrients back into the soil.

But living in such a wet and humid place comes with its challenges. Rainforest plants have evolved clever ways to deal with the constant rain. Many have leaves with drip tips—pointed ends that help water run off quickly, preventing it from pooling and causing rot. Others have thick, waxy coatings on their leaves to repel water and protect against fungal infections. These adaptations show just how resourceful rainforest plants can be in the face of such a unique climate.

Animals, too, have adapted to the rainforest's high rainfall and humidity. Birds like toucans and parrots have waterproof feathers that keep them dry during downpours. Mammals like sloths and jaguars often seek shelter under the dense canopy during heavy rains, while insects like ants and termites build water-resistant nests to protect their colonies. Even fish have adapted to the rainforest's climate—many species, like piranhas and catfish, live in the rivers and streams that swell with rainwater, making the most of the wet environment.

The rainforest's climate also affects the way sound travels. The thick, humid air carries sound incredibly well, which is why you can hear the calls of howler monkeys and the chirps of frogs from far away. This ability to communicate over long distances is important for many rainforest animals, especially those that need to find mates or warn each other of danger.

Despite the challenges, the rainforest's climate is what makes it one of the most biodiverse places on Earth. The constant rainfall and high humidity create a stable, warm environment where countless species can thrive. From the tallest trees in the emergent layer to the tiniest fungi on the forest floor, every part of the rainforest depends on its unique climate to survive.

Temperatures that stay warm year-round

Most tropical rainforests sit near the equator, the imaginary line that wraps around the middle of the Earth. Here, the sun shines almost directly overhead every day, delivering a steady stream of heat and light. Temperatures in the rainforest usually hover between 70 and 85 degrees Fahrenheit. While this might sound like perfect vacation weather, it's more than that—it's the foundation for a thriving ecosystem.

Warm temperatures mean that plants can grow year-round. There's no need to take a break during the winter because, in the rainforest, there isn't one. Trees are constantly producing leaves, flowers, and fruit. This never-ending cycle of growth supports countless animals, from insects that pollinate flowers to monkeys that feast on ripe fruit. In turn, these animals help plants spread their seeds and reproduce, keeping the cycle going.

Take a look at the towering trees in the rainforest, like the kapok or Brazil nut trees. These giants rely on the consistent warmth to grow tall and strong. Warm temperatures allow them to photosynthesize—the process of turning sunlight into food—every single day. This steady growth helps create the layers of the rainforest, from the shady understory to the sunlit canopy and the emergent layer above.

Warmth also affects the animals that call the rainforest home. Many rainforest creatures are cold-blooded, like reptiles and amphibians. Cold-blooded animals rely on their surroundings to regulate their body temperature, and the rainforest's warm, stable climate is perfect for them. Frogs, lizards, and snakes can stay active all year, hunting for food and finding mates without worrying about freezing temperatures.

For example, the poison dart frog thrives in the rainforest's warm and humid climate. Its brightly colored skin glistens as it hops among leaves, and the steady warmth keeps it agile and alert. Similarly, the emerald tree boa, a snake that coils itself around branches high in the trees, benefits from the warmth, which helps it digest its meals and remain ready to hunt.

Even mammals, like jaguars and sloths, rely on the rainforest's constant warmth. Warm temperatures mean that food is always available, whether it's a jaguar hunting for prey or a sloth munching on leaves. The consistent climate allows these animals to live their lives without the seasonal stresses that animals in colder regions face, like storing food or hibernating through the winter.

Birds, too, find the warm rainforest an ideal home. Parrots, toucans, and harpy eagles are active year-round, nesting and raising their young in the steady temperatures. The warmth also allows for the abundance of insects, a crucial food source for many birds. Without cold snaps to slow down their activity, insects thrive, buzzing, crawling, and flitting through the rainforest in every season.

The rainforest's warm temperatures also play a role in its famous humidity. Heat causes water to evaporate, and in a rainforest, that water often comes from the endless streams, rivers, and damp soil. As water evaporates, it adds moisture to the air, creating the humid environment that's so important to the rainforest's plants and animals. The warmth and humidity work together, creating a feedback loop that keeps the rainforest lush and vibrant.

For humans living in or visiting the rainforest, the warm climate can feel both comforting and challenging. The steady temperatures make it easier to grow crops and gather food from the forest, but the constant heat and humidity can also be exhausting. Indigenous peoples have adapted to this climate over generations, developing ways of life that make the most of what the rainforest offers while staying cool and comfortable.

How the climate shapes life in the rainforest

Rainforest trees don't just grow tall—they grow in layers, creating the distinct levels of the rainforest: the emergent layer, the canopy, the understory, and the forest floor. This layering isn't random; it's a direct result of the climate. With sunlight filtering down through the dense canopy, plants must adapt to either bask in the light above or make the most of the shade below. Some trees, like the towering kapok tree, rise above the canopy to soak up the most sunlight, while others, like ferns and mosses, thrive in the dim light closer to the ground.

The constant rain is another factor shaping the plants here. Rainforest trees have developed drip tips on their leaves, allowing water to run off quickly and avoid pooling. Without these adaptations, leaves could become waterlogged, making them vulnerable to rot or fungi. In this way, the heavy rainfall pushes plants to evolve clever designs to stay healthy and productive.

But it's not just the plants that have to adapt to the rainforest's climate—animals do too. Take a look at how insects, birds, and mammals interact with the rainforest's humidity and warmth. Frogs like the red-eyed tree frog rely on the damp air to keep their skin moist, which is essential for breathing. Without the rainforest's consistent humidity, these amphibians wouldn't survive. In the canopy, monkeys swing through the trees, feasting on fruits that grow year-round, a luxury made possible by the steady climate. Birds, such as toucans, benefit from an abundance of insects and fruits, which never disappear thanks to the constant rainfall and warm temperatures.

The water cycle in the rainforest isn't just about rain falling from the sky—it's a system that every living thing contributes to and depends on. Trees release water vapor through transpiration, which helps form clouds and brings rain back to the forest. This cycle creates a reliable supply of water, which in turn supports the streams, rivers, and pools that criss-cross the rainforest. These waterways provide a home for fish like piranhas, caimans, and other aquatic creatures, all of which play their part in the rainforest's complex web of life.

The warm, stable climate also allows animals to develop unique behaviors. Many species don't need to migrate or hibernate because food and shelter are available year-round. Sloths, for instance, spend their lives hanging in trees, moving slowly to conserve energy. In a colder or drier environment, their laid-back lifestyle might not work, but in the rainforest, it's perfectly suited to their surroundings. Jaguars, on the other hand, take advantage of the rainforest's rivers and dense vegetation to hunt, using the steady temperatures to stay active and agile.

The rainforest's climate even influences how animals communicate. The thick, humid air carries sound extremely well, which is why you can hear the deep roar of a howler monkey or the high-pitched chirp of a tree frog from far away. These calls are essential for finding mates, warning of danger, or simply claiming territory in a world teeming with life. Without the rainforest's unique climate, these sounds might not travel as far or as effectively.

Rainforest fungi and bacteria, too, owe much of their success to the climate. The constant warmth and moisture create the perfect conditions for decomposers to break down dead plants and animals, recycling nutrients back into the soil. This process is crucial for the health of the rainforest, allowing new plants to grow and supporting the entire ecosystem. In cooler or drier climates, decomposition happens much more slowly, but in the rainforest, it's a speedy process that keeps life moving forward.

Even the animals you might not expect to be influenced by the climate, like insects, are shaped by it in surprising ways. Army ants, for example, march through the rainforest in search of food, relying on the damp soil to create trails and the abundance of prey that thrives in the warm, wet environment. Butterflies and moths, with their delicate wings, find ample nectar from rainforest flowers, thanks to the year-round growth of plants supported by the climate.

And then there are the symbiotic relationships—the partnerships between species that are so common in the rainforest. The climate allows these relationships to flourish. Bromeliads collect rainwater in their cup-like leaves, creating small pools where frogs lay their eggs. Ants protect certain trees from herbivores in exchange for shelter and food. Even microorganisms, like nitrogen-fixing bacteria, form partnerships with plants to enrich the soil. These interactions wouldn't be possible without the rainforest's unique combination of rain, humidity, and warmth.

5

INDIGENOUS PEOPLES OF THE RAINFOREST

The rainforest isn't just home to towering trees and colorful animals—it's also a place where people have lived for thousands of years. Indigenous tribes, whose ancestors have called the rainforest home for generations, live deep within its green embrace. These communities are part of the rainforest, just as much as the plants and animals, and they've learned how to thrive in this unique environment in ways that many of us can only imagine.

Step into the world of an indigenous tribe, and you'll find a life closely tied to the forest. Every part of their day, from gathering food to building shelter, is shaped by their connection to nature. Many tribes don't just live in the rainforest—they live with it, taking only what they need and giving back by protecting the environment that sustains them. This balance is at the heart of their traditional ways of life.

One of the most well-known groups is the Yanomami, who live in the Amazon rainforest, straddling the borders of Brazil and Venezuela. The Yanomami build communal homes called shabonos, which are circular structures made from palm leaves, vines, and wood. These homes are designed to blend into the forest and provide shelter for several families. Inside a shabono, life revolves around sharing—meals, stories, and work are all done together, creating a strong sense of community.

Food for the Yanomami often comes from the forest itself. They gather fruits, nuts, and roots, hunt animals like monkeys and birds, and fish in the rivers. Hunting is done carefully, with respect for the animals and the forest. Instead of hunting more than they need, they take only what will feed their families, ensuring that the rainforest can continue to provide for future generations.

Another remarkable group is the Penan people of Borneo. They are known for their incredible skill as hunters and gatherers, relying on the rainforest for everything from food to medicine. The Penan use blowpipes made from bamboo to hunt small animals, like birds and monkeys. These blowpipes shoot tiny darts, often coated with natural poisons from plants. This method of hunting is silent and precise, allowing the Penan to move through the forest without disturbing its balance.

The Penan also have an extraordinary knowledge of the rainforest's plants. They use tree bark to make rope, leaves to weave baskets, and sap to treat wounds. For them, the rainforest is a giant, living pharmacy and hardware store combined. This deep understanding of the forest has been passed down through generations, with elders teaching children how to recognize useful plants and navigate the dense jungle.

In Papua New Guinea, the Huli people have built their lives around the rainforest's rhythm. Known for their colorful face paint and elaborate wigs made from human hair, the Huli live in small villages surrounded by gardens. They grow crops like sweet potatoes and taro, often using clever techniques to enrich the soil and ensure their gardens thrive in the rainforest's nutrient-poor ground. While farming provides much of their food, the Huli also hunt and fish, using spears and traps they've crafted from forest materials.

What's truly amazing about these tribes is how their ways of life are shaped by their respect for the rainforest. For many indigenous peoples, the forest isn't just a resource—it's sacred. They believe that spirits inhabit the trees, rivers, and animals, and that humans are just one part of a much larger, interconnected world. This belief influences how they interact with the forest, guiding them to live sustainably and avoid overusing its resources.

But life in the rainforest isn't without challenges. Insects like mosquitoes can spread diseases, and heavy rains can make travel difficult. Despite these hardships, indigenous tribes have developed tools and techniques to adapt. For example, some tribes use natural repellents made from plants to ward off mosquitoes, while others build raised platforms to keep their homes dry during floods.

Stories and traditions are another important part of life in the rainforest. Indigenous tribes often pass down their knowledge through oral storytelling, sharing tales of ancestors, animals, and spirits. These stories are more than just entertainment—they're lessons about survival, respect, and the natural world. They teach younger generations how to hunt, what plants to avoid, and why it's important to protect the forest.

For children growing up in these communities, the rainforest is their classroom. They learn to climb trees to pick fruit, paddle canoes through winding rivers, and track animals by reading the signs they leave behind. This hands-on education prepares them for a life in harmony with the forest, ensuring that the knowledge and traditions of their tribe continue to thrive.

How indigenous people use rainforest resources sustainably

One way indigenous people use the rainforest sustainably is by hunting and fishing with care. Instead of hunting every animal they see, they focus on specific species and avoid overhunting. For example, they might only hunt larger animals like peccaries or tapirs during certain times of the year, giving populations a chance to recover. When they fish, they often use traditional methods, like nets or traps made from natural materials, ensuring they don't catch more than their families need. By being selective and thoughtful, they help maintain the balance of the ecosystem.

Farming in the rainforest is another practice that reflects sustainability. You might think of farming as clearing large areas of land, but indigenous people often use a method called shifting cultivation, or "slash-and-burn." While this might sound destructive, it's done in a way that allows the forest to regenerate. A small patch of land is cleared and used for farming for a few years. Once the soil starts to lose nutrients, the area is left to rest and recover while the community moves to another spot. Over time, the forest regrows, and the cycle can begin again. This method avoids permanent damage and ensures that the rainforest remains healthy.

When it comes to gathering plants, indigenous

people have an incredible knowledge of what the forest offers. They know which fruits are ripe, which roots are ready to harvest, and which leaves can be used for medicine. They also know when to leave plants alone to allow them to grow and reproduce. For example, when collecting Brazil nuts, they only take the nuts that have naturally fallen to the ground, leaving the ones still on the trees to grow into future generations of trees. This kind of mindful harvesting helps preserve the forest's resources.

Many indigenous groups have a spiritual connection to the rainforest, which influences how they use its resources. They see the forest as a living being, filled with spirits and energy, and they believe that harming the forest without reason can upset this balance. This belief fosters a deep respect for the land, guiding them to use its resources carefully and only when necessary. For instance, when a tree is cut down to build a canoe, the act is often accompanied by rituals or prayers to honor the tree and thank it for its contribution.

Medicine is another area where indigenous people use the rainforest sustainably. The forest is like a giant pharmacy, filled with plants that can treat everything from fevers to wounds. Indigenous healers, often called shamans, have an extensive knowledge of medicinal plants, passed down through generations. They use bark, leaves, roots, and flowers to create remedies, but they're careful not to overharvest. They know that taking too much of a plant could wipe it out, so they only gather what they need and often leave offerings as a sign of gratitude.

Shelter and tools are also made sustainably. Houses are built using materials like palm leaves, vines, and bamboo, which are gathered without causing permanent damage. These materials are light-weight and biodegradable, blending seamlessly into the environment. Tools, like fishing spears or baskets, are crafted from natural resources and are often repaired or reused instead of being discarded. This approach minimizes waste and ensures that the rain-forest remains a source of materials for future generations.

Even the way indigenous people share knowledge reflects sustainability. Children learn from their elders by observing and participating in daily activities, from gathering food to weaving baskets. This hands-on learning helps pass down traditions and ensures that the younger generation understands the importance of caring for the rainforest. It's not just about knowing how to use resources—it's about understanding the balance between taking and giving back.

One fascinating example of sustainable living comes from the Kayapo people in the Amazon. They've developed a unique way of planting crops in the forest by creating "forest islands." These are small clearings surrounded by natural vegetation where they grow a mix of crops like cassava, bananas, and maize. By planting a variety of species together, they mimic the diversity of the rainforest, which helps keep the soil healthy and reduces the need for chemical fertilizers. This method allows them to farm without destroying the surrounding forest.

Another example is the use of "living pharmacies." Instead of cutting down a tree for its bark or roots, some tribes will plant seeds from the tree near their homes. This way, they have access to the medicine they need without harming the original plant. Over time, these living pharmacies grow into gardens that provide food, medicine, and shelter for both people and animals.

Indigenous peoples also play a crucial role in protecting the rainforest. They are often the first to notice changes in the environment, like a decrease in certain animal populations or signs of deforestation. By working with conservation groups, they help monitor and defend the rainforest, using their traditional knowledge to guide sustainable practices. Their efforts benefit not just their communities, but the entire planet, as the rainforest plays a critical role in regulating the Earth's climate.

6

THE RAINFOREST'S ROLE IN THE WORLD

Rainforest trees are like natural pumps, pulling water from the ground and releasing it into the air. How do they do this? Through a process called transpiration. Each tree has roots that suck up water from the soil. This water travels through the tree, eventually reaching the leaves. When the leaves release tiny droplets of water vapor into the air, it's called transpiration. Imagine millions of trees doing this at the same time. It's like the entire rainforest is breathing out mist, creating a thick, humid atmosphere.

But the rainforest isn't just releasing water into the air—it's also helping to form rain. As the water vapor rises, it cools and condenses into clouds. These clouds grow heavier and heavier until they release the water back down as rain. This process, called precipitation, is what keeps the rainforest wet and green. What's amazing is that much of the rain that falls in the rainforest is actually recycled water—water that was released by the trees in the first place.

This means the rainforest is a self-sustaining system. The trees release water, the water forms clouds, and the clouds bring rain back to the forest. Without this cycle, the rainforest couldn't survive. And the rainforest doesn't just keep this water cycle going for itself—it also affects areas far beyond its borders. Moisture from the rainforest can travel great distances, helping to bring rain to nearby regions and even to places thousands of miles away.

The Amazon rainforest, for example, is so massive that it's sometimes called the "lungs of the Earth" because of its role in producing oxygen. But it's also like the Earth's water heart, pumping moisture into the atmosphere and helping to regulate weather patterns across South America and beyond. Some of the rain that falls in the Andes Mountains, or even on distant plains, can be traced back to water vapor released by the trees of the Amazon.

But it's not just the trees that contribute to the water cycle—plants of all sizes play a part. Mosses and ferns that carpet the forest floor, vines that twist their way through the canopy, and even the tiny orchids clinging to tree branches all release water vapor. Together, they create an environment where rain is a constant presence, feeding rivers, streams, and the countless creatures that depend on them.

The rainforest's ability to produce rain is also connected to its incredible biodiversity. Plants and animals work together to keep the water cycle running smoothly. Take the giant trees, for example. Their massive canopies provide shade that keeps the forest floor cool and damp, reducing evaporation and helping the soil hold onto water. This moist soil supports smaller plants, which in turn release their own water vapor, adding to the cycle.

Animals also play their part. When birds and monkeys eat fruit, they scatter seeds across the forest. These seeds grow into new plants, which eventually join the water cycle. Even the movement of animals, like jaguars prowling through the underbrush or herds of tapirs splashing in rivers, stirs up the environment, helping water seep into the ground and keeping the system dynamic and alive.

Rainforest rivers are another crucial piece of the puzzle. These winding waterways carry rainwater from the forest to the ocean, connecting the rainforest to the broader global water cycle. Along the way, they support countless forms of life, from fish and amphibians to the people who live along their banks. The mighty Amazon River, for instance, begins as tiny streams in the Andes Mountains, fed by rain from the forest. It grows into one of the largest rivers in the world, carrying freshwater across thousands of miles before it reaches the Atlantic Ocean.

Rainforests even help stabilize the climate by cooling the air. As water evaporates from the leaves of trees and plants, it absorbs heat, creating a natural cooling effect. This doesn't just benefit the rainforest itself—it influences global temperatures, helping to regulate the Earth's climate.

The Rainforest and the Air

The air that fills your lungs is full of oxygen, the invisible gas that keeps us alive. But where does all that oxygen come from? You might be surprised to learn that a huge part of it comes from plants, especially those in the rainforest. The rainforest isn't just a home for amazing animals and towering trees—it's like a giant air factory, working tirelessly to produce oxygen and clean the air by absorbing carbon dioxide. It's a job the rainforest has been doing for millions of years, and it's one of the many reasons why it's so important to the planet.

Imagine a single leaf on a rainforest tree, high up in the canopy where sunlight streams down. That leaf is like a tiny solar panel, capturing the sun's energy and using it to power an incredible process called photosynthesis. During photosynthesis, the leaf takes in carbon dioxide—a gas that we breathe out and that's also released by burning fuels—and uses sunlight to transform it into sugar, which the tree uses as food. But here's the best part: as the leaf makes food for the tree, it releases oxygen back into the air.

Now multiply that single leaf by the millions and millions of leaves in the rainforest. Each one is quietly working, pulling in carbon dioxide and releasing oxygen, like billions of tiny green machines. Together, they create a massive supply of fresh oxygen, not just for the animals and people living in the rainforest, but for the entire planet.

This is why the Amazon rainforest is often called the "lungs of the Earth." It produces a significant portion of the oxygen in our atmosphere, helping to keep the planet's air breathable. But the rainforest doesn't just give us oxygen—it also helps balance the levels of carbon dioxide, a gas that contributes to global warming when there's too much of it in the atmosphere.

Carbon dioxide comes from all sorts of sources: car engines, factories, power plants, and even forest fires. When there's too much carbon dioxide in the air, it traps heat, causing the Earth's temperature to rise. This is called the greenhouse effect, and it's one of the main drivers of climate change. The rainforest helps combat this problem by acting as a giant carbon sponge. Trees and plants absorb carbon dioxide during photosynthesis, storing it in their trunks, branches, leaves, and roots. This process is known as carbon sequestration, and it's a powerful tool for slowing down climate change.

Imagine a single tree in the rainforest. Over its lifetime, it might absorb hundreds or even thousands of pounds of carbon dioxide. Now imagine an entire rainforest filled with these carbon-absorbing giants. Together, they act like a giant vacuum cleaner, sucking carbon dioxide out of the air and locking it away. This helps keep the Earth's atmosphere stable and protects us from the worst effects of global warming.

But the rainforest's role doesn't end there. It also plays a part in regulating the air's overall quality. Plants in the rainforest release not just oxygen but also water vapor, which helps cool the air and keeps the atmosphere healthy. The rainforest even produces tiny particles called aerosols, which can help form clouds and bring rain to surrounding areas.

The connection between the rainforest and the air we breathe is so strong that when forests are destroyed, it affects the entire planet. Cutting down trees releases the carbon stored in their wood back into the atmosphere, adding more carbon dioxide and speeding up climate change. It also reduces the amount of oxygen being produced, making the air less fresh and healthy.

When large areas of rainforest are cleared for farming, logging, or mining, the balance between oxygen and carbon dioxide in the atmosphere is disrupted. Scientists call this deforestation, and it's one of the biggest threats to the rainforest and the planet. Without enough trees to absorb carbon dioxide and produce oxygen, the Earth's air becomes harder to breathe and less able to regulate temperature.

Indigenous peoples living in the rainforest understand how vital these trees are, not just for their own survival but for the health of the entire world. Many of their stories and traditions emphasize the importance of protecting trees and using the forest's resources responsibly. By living in harmony with the rainforest, they help ensure that it can continue its role as the planet's air factory.

Rainforests as the planet's "lungs"

To understand why rainforests are so important to the Earth's atmosphere, let's start with the incredible process of photosynthesis. Plants, including the towering trees of the rainforest, use sunlight, water, and carbon dioxide to make their own food. During this process, they release oxygen as a byproduct. It's like a magical exchange: they take in something we can't use (carbon dioxide) and give us something we can't live without (oxygen). This exchange happens on a massive scale in the rainforest because of the sheer number of plants packed into its dense, green world.

Imagine a single tree. Its leaves are like little factories, each one working hard to absorb carbon dioxide and release oxygen. Now multiply that by the billions of trees in the Amazon rainforest alone, not to mention all the other rainforests around the world. Together, these forests produce a huge portion of the world's oxygen. While oceans are actually the largest producers of oxygen, thanks to tiny organisms called phytoplankton, rainforests still play a crucial role in maintaining the balance of gases in our atmosphere.

But the rainforest's role as the planet's lungs doesn't stop with producing oxygen. It also acts as a giant air filter. By absorbing carbon dioxide, rainforests help slow the effects of global warming. Carbon dioxide is a greenhouse gas, meaning it traps heat in the atmosphere. When there's too much of it, the planet starts to heat up, leading to climate change. Rainforests, with their dense vegetation, act like sponges, soaking up excess carbon dioxide and keeping the air cleaner and cooler.

Let's take a closer look at how this works. When trees grow, they store carbon in their trunks, branches, and roots. This process, known as carbon sequestration, locks carbon away, preventing it from contributing to the greenhouse effect. A single mature tree can store hundreds of pounds of carbon dioxide over its lifetime. Imagine what billions of trees in the rainforest are capable of! They're like a giant safety net, protecting us from the worst effects of climate change.

This balancing act between oxygen production and carbon absorption is one of the reasons rainforests are often compared to lungs. Just as your lungs take in air and deliver oxygen to your body, rainforests take in carbon dioxide and provide oxygen to the planet. But unlike your lungs, which are confined to your chest, the rainforest's "breathing" extends across entire continents, affecting ecosystems and climates far beyond its borders.

Rainforests also help regulate the air's temperature and moisture levels. As trees release water vapor through their leaves, they cool the air around them and add humidity to the atmosphere. This process not only helps create the rainforest's characteristic misty environment but also contributes to global weather patterns. The Amazon rainforest, for instance, influences rainfall as far away as the United States. It's not just a regional powerhouse—it's a global one.

The idea of the rainforest as the planet's lungs isn't just a poetic metaphor; it's a reminder of how interconnected life on Earth truly is. When forests are cut down, the balance is disrupted. Trees that once absorbed carbon dioxide and produced oxygen are no longer there to do their job. Worse, the carbon stored in those trees is released back into the atmosphere, adding to the problem of global warming. Deforestation turns the planet's lungs from a life-giving force into a source of pollution.

But the story of the rainforest as the Earth's lungs isn't all about danger and loss. It's also a story of hope and resilience. Rainforests are incredibly good at bouncing back when given the chance. When deforested areas are allowed to regrow, the new trees begin their work of absorbing carbon dioxide and releasing oxygen, slowly healing the damage. Conservation efforts around the world are helping protect existing rainforests and restore degraded ones, ensuring they can continue their vital role.

7

THREATS TO THE RAINFOREST

Imagine a rainforest full of towering trees. They create a canopy so dense that sunlight barely reaches the forest floor. Birds chirp, monkeys swing from branch to branch, and the air smells rich and earthy. Now imagine a bulldozer cutting through this lush environment, knocking down trees one after another. Where once there was vibrant green life, there's now an open patch of land, bare and lifeless. This is deforestation—when large areas of forest are cleared, often for farming, cattle grazing, or building roads and cities.

One major cause of deforestation is agriculture. As the world's population grows, people need more food, and rainforests are often cleared to make space for crops like soybeans or for cattle pastures. For example, in the Amazon rainforest, vast areas are being turned into farmland. The process starts with logging—cutting down valuable hardwood trees to sell for furniture, paper, and other products. Once the trees are gone, the land is often burned to clear away the remaining vegetation. This is called slash-and-burn farming, and while it provides short-term benefits, it has devastating long-term effects.

The problem with cutting down trees isn't just that the forest looks different—it's what those trees do for the planet. Remember how rainforests act like the Earth's lungs, producing oxygen and absorbing carbon dioxide? When trees are cut down, they can no longer perform this vital function. Even worse, the carbon they've stored is released back into the atmosphere, contributing to climate change. It's like poking holes in a life jacket—it may not sink you immediately, but over time, the damage adds up.

Logging, a major part of deforestation, is a complicated issue. On one hand, wood is an important resource. People use it to build homes, make furniture, and create paper products. In some cases, logging is done responsibly, with efforts to replant trees and minimize damage. This is called sustainable logging. But in many parts of the rainforest, illegal logging is a huge problem. Trees are cut down without permission, often in protected areas, and without any plans to replace them.

Illegal logging isn't just bad for the environment—

it's bad for the people who depend on the rainforest. Indigenous communities, who have lived in harmony with the forest for generations, often lose their homes and resources when logging companies move in. Animals, too, are displaced. A single fallen tree can destroy the habitat of countless creatures, from birds nesting in the canopy to insects living in the bark.

The ripple effects of deforestation and logging extend far beyond the rainforest. When trees are cut down, the soil becomes exposed to heavy rains. Without roots to hold it in place, the soil is washed away, causing erosion. Rivers can become clogged with sediment, affecting fish and other aquatic life. Nearby communities might lose access to clean water, and the land becomes less fertile, making it harder for new plants to grow.

Deforestation also affects the rainforest's ability to regulate the water cycle. Trees release water vapor into the air through transpiration, helping to form clouds and bring rain. When large areas of forest are cleared, this process is disrupted, leading to less rainfall. In some cases, the lack of rain can turn once-lush areas into dry, barren landscapes. This is called desertification, and it's a stark reminder of how fragile the balance of the rainforest really is.

But it's not all bad news. Around the world, people are working to protect rainforests and fight deforestation. Conservation groups are raising awareness about the importance of rainforests and pushing for stronger laws to prevent illegal logging. Some countries are creating protected areas where logging and farming are banned, allowing the forest to recover. Indigenous communities are also playing a key role, using their traditional knowledge to manage and protect the rainforest.

One promising solution is sustainable forestry. This involves cutting down trees in a way that allows the forest to regenerate. For example, loggers might only cut a certain number of trees in a specific area, leaving enough behind to keep the ecosystem intact. They might also replant trees to replace the ones they've taken. While it's not a perfect solution, sustainable forestry is a step in the right direction.

Another way to fight deforestation is by reducing the demand for rainforest products. By choosing recycled paper, buying wood from sustainable sources, and avoiding products made with palm oil—a common ingredient linked to deforestation—consumers can make a big difference. Even small actions, like supporting companies that prioritize environmental responsibility, help protect the rainforest.

Reforestation, or planting new trees in deforested areas, is another strategy to restore the rainforest. While it takes time for new trees to grow, reforestation can help bring back lost habitats and improve the health of the ecosystem. Some organizations even involve local communities in reforestation efforts, providing jobs and education while helping the rainforest recover.

Agriculture and palm oil plantations

As the world's population grows, so does the need for food. Farmers need more space to grow crops like soybeans, corn, and rice. Often, the land they clear for farming is part of the rainforest. Trees are cut down, animals are forced to leave, and the once-lush forest becomes farmland. While farming is essential for feeding people, the way it's done can cause long-term damage to the environment.

One major issue is slash-and-burn farming. This technique involves cutting down trees and burning the remaining vegetation to make the land ready for crops. At first, it seems like a good idea. The ashes from the burned plants add nutrients to the soil, making it fertile. But rainforest soil isn't like the soil in other places. It's thin and loses nutrients quickly. After a few years of farming, the land becomes useless, and farmers move on to clear another part of the forest. This cycle leaves behind large patches of land that take years to recover—if they recover at all.

Agriculture doesn't just affect the land—it also changes the water and air. Without trees, the soil becomes exposed to heavy rains, which wash it away into rivers. This runoff can clog waterways with mud, harming fish and other aquatic life. Meanwhile, burning trees releases carbon dioxide into the atmosphere, contributing to climate change. The forest, once a carbon sponge that helped cool the Earth, becomes a source of greenhouse gases.

Among the crops grown in former rainforests, palm oil is one of the most controversial. Palm oil comes from the fruit of the oil palm tree, and it's used in many everyday products—everything from cookies and ice cream to shampoo and soap. It's popular because it's cheap to produce, but growing it often comes at the expense of the rainforest.

Palm oil plantations are massive. Picture rows of identical trees stretching as far as the eye can see, planted where a diverse, vibrant rainforest once stood. To create these plantations, companies clear large areas of forest, cutting down trees and burning whatever is left. Animals lose their habitats, rivers are polluted, and the balance of the ecosystem is destroyed.

One of the most heartbreaking consequences of palm oil plantations is the impact on wildlife. Orangutans, which live in the rainforests of Borneo and Sumatra, are among the hardest hit. These gentle, intelligent creatures depend on the forest for food and shelter. When their homes are destroyed, they're left with nowhere to go. Many are killed or captured, and their populations are shrinking fast. Tigers, elephants, and countless other species face similar dangers.

Palm oil plantations also affect people. Indigenous communities, who have lived in the rainforest for generations, are often forced to leave their land to make way for plantations. They lose not just their homes, but their way of life, which is deeply connected to the forest. This creates conflicts between local communities and large companies, with many people fighting to protect their rights and their environment.

But why is palm oil so widespread? The answer lies in its versatility. Palm oil is used in a huge variety of products because it's cheap, efficient, and easy to grow. A single oil palm tree produces more oil than other crops like soybeans or sunflowers, making it an attractive choice for companies. The demand for palm oil has skyrocketed over the years, driving more deforestation as companies rush to meet the global need.

Despite its environmental toll, there are efforts to make palm oil production more sustainable. Some organizations are working with companies to develop certifications for palm oil that's grown without destroying the rainforest. These certifications help consumers identify products made with responsibly sourced palm oil. While it's not a perfect solution, it's a step toward balancing the need for palm oil with the need to protect the rainforest.

There are also innovative farming practices that aim to reduce the damage caused by agriculture. Agro-forestry, for example, involves growing crops alongside trees instead of clearing the forest completely. This method allows farmers to grow food while preserving the ecosystem. It also provides homes for wildlife and helps maintain the rainforest's role in the water and carbon cycles.

Climate change and its impact on rainforests

Climate change begins with the release of greenhouse gases, like carbon dioxide and methane, into the atmosphere. These gases trap heat, causing the Earth's temperature to rise. While a small increase might not seem like a big deal, even tiny shifts in temperature can have a huge effect on ecosystems like the rainforest, where life is finely tuned to thrive in specific conditions.

One of the most noticeable impacts of climate change on rainforests is the change in rainfall patterns. The rainforest gets its name because it depends on a steady supply of rain. Water evaporates from the leaves of trees, rises into the atmosphere, and eventually falls back as rain. This cycle keeps the forest lush and green. But as temperatures rise, this delicate cycle is thrown off balance.

In some areas, rainforests are experiencing longer dry seasons and less frequent rainfall. Imagine the soil becoming dusty and cracked, streams shrinking into puddles, and plants struggling to find enough water to survive. Without enough rain, trees can't perform photosynthesis as efficiently, which means less oxygen is produced and less carbon dioxide is absorbed. The entire ecosystem starts to weaken.

At the same time, other areas face the opposite problem: too much rain in a short period. Intense storms can cause flooding, washing away soil and destroying habitats. Rivers can overflow, forcing animals to flee and disrupting the lives of indigenous communities. Whether it's too little rain or too much, the changes brought by climate change make life in the rainforest increasingly unpredictable.

Higher temperatures also take a toll on the plants and animals that call the rainforest home. Many species in the rainforest are specially adapted to live within a narrow range of temperatures. When the climate becomes hotter, some plants may struggle to grow, and animals may have difficulty finding food or shelter. For example, frogs, which rely on the rainforest's constant humidity to keep their skin moist, might face challenges as the air becomes drier. Birds that depend on specific flowering plants for nectar might lose their food sources if those plants bloom less often.

Wildfires, which are rare in rainforests under normal conditions, are becoming more common due to climate change. Higher temperatures and longer dry seasons create the perfect conditions for fires to start and spread. These fires can destroy vast areas of forest, killing plants and animals and releasing massive amounts of carbon dioxide into the atmosphere. It's a vicious cycle: climate change makes fires more likely, and fires contribute to even more climate change.

Coral reefs and polar ice caps often get a lot of attention when people talk about climate change, but rainforests are just as vulnerable—and just as important to protect. The Amazon rainforest, for instance, is so vast and so full of life that it's often called a "carbon sink," meaning it absorbs more carbon dioxide than it releases. But as deforestation and climate change weaken the Amazon, it risks becoming a carbon source, releasing more carbon dioxide than it absorbs. This shift could accelerate global warming, affecting ecosystems around the world.

One of the most alarming effects of climate change on rainforests is the threat of a tipping point. A tipping point is like a line that, once crossed, causes dramatic and often irreversible changes. Scientists worry that if too much of the rainforest is destroyed or if the climate becomes too dry, the rainforest could transform into a savanna—a much drier ecosystem with fewer trees and less biodiversity. This would not only be devastating for the animals and plants that depend on the rainforest, but it would also have global consequences, including less oxygen production and faster climate change.

Despite these challenges, the rainforest remains resilient, and there are ways to help protect it. One of the most effective strategies is reducing greenhouse gas emissions. This means burning less fossil fuel, using renewable energy sources like solar and wind power, and protecting forests from deforestation. Every effort to reduce carbon dioxide in the atmosphere helps slow climate change and gives the rainforest a better chance to adapt.

Endangered species and loss of biodiversity

Biodiversity is a big word that simply means the variety of life in a place. Rainforests are the most biodiverse places on Earth, home to millions of species of plants, animals, fungi, and microorganisms. Some of these species are found nowhere else in the world, making the rainforest incredibly special. But this rich tapestry of life is under threat. Deforestation, climate change, hunting, and illegal wildlife trade are pushing many rainforest species to the brink of extinction.

Take the orangutan, for example. These gentle, intelligent primates live in the rainforests of Borneo and Sumatra. They spend most of their time in the trees, swinging from branch to branch and eating fruits like durians and mangos. But as palm oil plantations and logging destroy their habitat, orangutans are left with nowhere to live and nothing to eat. Many are injured or killed when they come into contact with humans, and their populations are shrinking rapidly.

Then there's the harpy eagle, a majestic bird of prey that soars through the Amazon rainforest. Known for its striking appearance and powerful talons, the harpy eagle plays a key role in keeping the rainforest's ecosystem in balance by hunting small mammals like sloths and monkeys. But as deforestation reduces the number of tall trees where harpy eagles build their nests, their numbers are dwindling.

Even tiny creatures face big threats. Poison dart frogs, with their brightly colored skin, are among the most iconic animals of the rainforest. Their vibrant hues warn predators of the toxic chemicals in their bodies. These frogs depend on the humid environment of the rainforest to survive, but climate change and habitat destruction are making it harder for them to find the right conditions to thrive.

The loss of biodiversity doesn't just affect individual species—it disrupts the entire ecosystem. Think of the rainforest as a giant web, with every plant, animal, and microorganism connected. When one strand of the web is cut, the whole structure weakens. For example, if a pollinator like a bee or butterfly disappears, the plants it pollinates might not be able to reproduce. This affects the animals that eat those plants, and the ripple effects can spread throughout the entire ecosystem.

Predators, in particular, play a crucial role in the rainforest. Jaguars, for instance, help keep populations of herbivores like deer and capybaras in check. Without predators, these herbivores could overgraze, damaging the forest floor and making it harder for new plants to grow. When a top predator is lost, it creates a domino effect that can lead to the collapse of entire ecosystems.

Humans, too, are affected by the loss of biodiversity in the rainforest. Many of the medicines we use today come from rainforest plants. Scientists study the chemicals in these plants to develop treatments for diseases like cancer, malaria, and diabetes. But when species go extinct, we lose not just the plants and animals themselves, but the potential discoveries they could have brought us.

Illegal hunting and wildlife trade are also major threats to rainforest species. Some animals are hunted for their meat, while others are captured and sold as exotic pets. Parrots, for instance, are often taken from the wild for their beautiful feathers and ability to mimic human speech. This not only reduces their populations in the wild but also disrupts their role in spreading seeds and maintaining the forest's health.

Despite these challenges, there's hope. Conservation efforts around the world are working to protect endangered species and preserve rainforest biodiversity. National parks and wildlife reserves provide safe habitats for animals, while breeding programs help boost populations of critically endangered species. Scientists are also studying how different species interact, learning more about how to restore ecosystems and prevent further loss.

Indigenous communities play a vital role in protecting biodiversity. Their traditional knowledge and sustainable practices help maintain the delicate balance of the rainforest. By working with conservation organizations and governments, they are helping to safeguard their forests and the countless species that depend on them.

8

PROTECTING THE RAINFOREST

The rainforest is often described as a treasure chest of life, filled with plants, animals, and ecosystems unlike anywhere else on Earth. To protect this treasure, people around the world have come up with creative and powerful ways to keep the rainforest safe. Some of the most important strategies involve setting aside land as national parks and reserves, as well as launching reforestation projects to bring back trees and habitats that have been lost. Each of these efforts is like a piece of a puzzle, working together to protect the rainforest for generations to come.

Take Yasuni National Park in Ecuador, for example. This park is one of the most biodiverse places on Earth, home to jaguars, pink river dolphins, and tiny frogs the size of your thumbnail. By setting aside this land as a national park, Ecuador has ensured that these species have a safe place to live, even as the surrounding rainforest faces threats. But protecting such a vast area isn't easy. Rangers patrol the park to keep it safe from illegal activities like poaching or logging, and researchers study the ecosystems to learn how to better protect them.

Reserves are another type of protected area, often managed by indigenous communities or conservation organizations. These areas may not have the same level of government protection as national parks, but they play a crucial role in conservation. In Brazil, the Chico Mendes Extractive Reserve is a place where people can harvest resources like rubber and Brazil nuts in a way that doesn't harm the forest. This approach, called sustainable use, allows people to benefit from the rainforest while keeping it intact.

Technology is helping make protected areas even more effective. Satellite imagery lets conservationists monitor large tracts of rainforest, spotting deforestation or illegal activities in real-time. Drones can fly over hard-to-reach areas, capturing detailed photos and videos to help researchers understand what's happening on the ground. With these tools, protecting national parks and reserves becomes more like solving a mystery, using clues from above to track changes and respond quickly.

While national parks and reserves protect existing

forests, reforestation projects focus on bringing back what's been lost. Imagine a barren patch of land, stripped of its trees and life. Now picture a group of people planting tiny saplings, each one a promise of a future forest. Reforestation is about more than just planting trees—it's about restoring ecosystems. The goal is to bring back the plants, animals, and cycles that make the rainforest such a vibrant, living system.

In Costa Rica, reforestation efforts have turned once-deforested areas into thriving rainforests. Over the past few decades, the country has invested heavily in planting trees and protecting its natural resources. Today, nearly half of Costa Rica is covered in forest, much of it restored through reforestation. These efforts have not only brought back wildlife but have also boosted eco-tourism, with visitors coming from around the world to experience the rainforest.

Reforestation projects can also involve local communities. In Indonesia, for example, farmers are working with conservation groups to replant areas of rainforest that were cleared for palm oil plantations. By planting native trees and crops that provide income without destroying the forest, these projects help people and the environment thrive together. It's a reminder that conservation isn't just about protecting nature—it's about finding solutions that work for everyone.

One of the most exciting aspects of reforestation is

the way it brings wildlife back to the rainforest. As trees grow, they create habitats for birds, monkeys, and other animals. In Brazil's Atlantic Forest, reforestation projects have helped restore corridors—strips of forest that connect isolated patches. These corridors allow animals to move freely, find food, and mate, increasing their chances of survival. It's like building bridges for wildlife, reconnecting the web of life in the rainforest.

Reforestation also helps combat climate change. Trees absorb carbon dioxide from the atmosphere, storing it in their trunks, branches, and roots. By planting more trees, reforestation projects act like a giant sponge, soaking up greenhouse gases and reducing the impact of global warming. In some cases, reforestation is even used as part of carbon offset programs, where companies pay to plant trees to balance out their emissions.

How kids can help

Recycling is like giving materials a second chance to be useful instead of throwing them away. For example, a cardboard box can be recycled into another box, or a plastic bottle can be turned into a backpack or a park bench. This might not seem directly related to the rainforest, but it actually helps in a big way. Recycling reduces the need to cut down trees for paper and card-board or to drill for oil to make new plastic. By recycling, you're helping reduce the demand for raw materials, which means fewer forests need to be cleared.

You can start recycling at home by separating materials like paper, plastic, glass, and metal into bins. If you're not sure what can be recycled, check with your local recycling program—they often have guides to help. At school, you can encourage your classmates and teachers to recycle too. Maybe your classroom can have a special recycling bin for paper, or your school can start a recycling club. Every piece of paper or bottle that gets recycled makes a difference.

Supporting sustainable products is another powerful way to help the rainforest. Sustainable products are made in ways that don't harm the environment. For example, some paper products are made from recycled paper or from wood that comes from forests managed responsibly. These forests are replanted after trees are cut down, ensuring they can continue to grow and provide habitats for animals.

One product that's often linked to rainforest destruction is palm oil. Palm oil is used in a lot of things, like cookies, candy, and shampoo, but its production can lead to deforestation. The good news is that there are companies that produce palm oil responsibly, without harming the rainforest. Look for products with labels that say "certified sustainable palm oil" or similar phrases. By choosing these products, you're sending a message that you care about the rainforest.

You can also shop for items made from bamboo, which grows quickly and can be harvested without damaging the environment. Bamboo is used to make everything from clothing to toothbrushes, and it's a great alternative to materials that might contribute to deforestation.

When it comes to food, buying local and organic can help too. Local food doesn't have to travel as far to reach your plate, which reduces pollution. Organic food is grown without harmful chemicals, which helps protect the soil and water. While not all local or organic food is directly linked to rainforest conservation, these choices are part of a bigger effort to live in a way that's kind to the planet.

Raising awareness is one of the most important things you can do to protect the rainforest. Think about all the amazing things you've learned about rainforests—the towering trees, the colorful animals, and the important role they play in keeping the planet healthy. Not everyone knows how special the rainforest is or what they can do to help. By sharing what you've learned, you can inspire others to care about the rainforest too.

You might start by talking to your family and friends. Tell them about how recycling helps reduce the need to cut down trees or why choosing sustainable products matters. You could even host a rainforest day at school, where everyone learns about the rainforest through games, videos, and activities. Maybe you could create a poster or a slideshow about the animals that live there or the dangers of deforestation.

If you like being creative, you could write a story or a poem about the rainforest, draw a picture of your favorite rainforest animal, or make a video explaining why rainforests are important. Sharing your creations online or at school is a great way to spread the word and get others involved.

Another way to raise awareness is by supporting organizations that protect the rainforest. Many conservation groups rely on donations to fund their work, but you don't have to have money to help. You could organize a fundraiser, like a bake sale or a car wash, and donate the proceeds to a group that's working to save the rainforest. Or you could volunteer your time to help out at local events or campaigns.

9

RAINFOREST WONDERS

S cientists estimate that about 10% of all the known species on Earth live in this rainforest. That means for every ten animals, plants, or fungi you can think of, at least one comes from the Amazon. Some of these creatures are well-known, like jaguars, sloths, and toucans, but many are still waiting to be discovered. In fact, researchers find new species in the Amazon all the time—brightly colored frogs, plants with healing properties, and even fish that can glow in the dark.

ONE OF THE most mysterious animals of the Amazon is the pink river dolphin, also known as the boto. These dolphins are unlike any other in the world. They live in the rivers and flooded forests of the Amazon, where their pale pink color makes them look like something out of a dream. Legends say that pink river dolphins can transform into humans at night and walk among the villages, adding to their air of mystery. Scientists are still learning about these incredible creatures, including how their flexible necks help them navigate through tangled underwater forests.

SPEAKING OF RIVERS, the Amazon River is another wonder of this incredible rainforest. It's the second-longest river in the world, stretching over 4,000 miles, and it carries more water than any other river. In fact, during the rainy season, the river can grow so wide that it looks more like an ocean. The Amazon River is home to a dizzying variety of fish, including the infamous piranha. While piranhas have a reputation for being fierce, they're usually harmless to humans unless provoked. They're more likely to feast on plants, insects, and dead animals than on anything alive.

THE AMAZON ISN'T JUST a home for animals—it's also a treasure chest of plants. Towering kapok trees, which can grow as tall as a 20-story building, dominate the canopy. These giants are sometimes called "emergent" trees because they rise above the rest of the forest, offering a view of the vast green expanse. Then there are plants like the Victoria amazonica, a type of water lily with leaves so large they can support the weight of a small child. Imagine stepping onto a giant, floating lily pad—it's like something out of a fairytale.

BUT THE AMAZON'S plants aren't just beautiful—they're also incredibly useful. Many of the medicines we use today come from plants that grow in the rainforest. For example, quinine, a treatment for malaria, was discovered in the bark of a tree found in the Amazon. Scientists believe there are countless other plants in the rainforest with potential cures for diseases, but many are still waiting to be studied. This is one of the reasons protecting the Amazon is so important—it holds secrets that could save lives.

THE AMAZON also has its fair share of mysteries. Deep within the rainforest, archaeologists have found evidence of ancient civilizations that lived there thousands of years ago. These people didn't just survive in the rainforest—they thrived, creating complex societies with roads, villages, and even what some scientists believe were early forms of agriculture. One of the most intriguing discoveries is a series of enormous earthworks called geoglyphs. These shapes, carved into the ground, are so large that they can only be seen from the air. No one knows exactly why they were made, but some believe they had religious or ceremonial significance.

ANOTHER MYSTERY of the Amazon is its "blackwater" rivers. Unlike the brown, muddy waters of the Amazon River, blackwater rivers are crystal clear with a dark, tea-like color. This happens because the water flows through forests rich in decaying leaves, which release tannins that stain the water. Despite their eerie appearance, these rivers are teeming with life, from fish to insects to aquatic plants.

THE AMAZON also plays a huge role in shaping the Earth's climate. Often called the "lungs of the Earth," the rainforest produces oxygen and absorbs carbon dioxide, helping regulate the planet's atmosphere. But the Amazon does more than that—it also creates its own weather. Trees in the rainforest release water vapor into the air, which helps form clouds and produce rain. This cycle keeps the Amazon lush and green, but it also affects weather patterns far beyond

South America, influencing rainfall as far away as the United States.

Rare species discovered recently

The rainforest is like a treasure chest that never runs out of surprises. Every time scientists explore its depths, they find new and astonishing species— plants, animals, and even fungi that no one has ever seen before. These discoveries aren't just fascinating; they remind us how much we still have to learn about the natural world. Some of these newly discovered species are so unique that they seem almost magical, as if the rainforest itself were a real-life fantasy land.

IMAGINE trekking through the Amazon rainforest with a team of scientists. The air is thick with humidity, and the sunlight filters through the dense canopy above. Suddenly, you hear someone shout. They've spotted something extraordinary—a tiny frog, no bigger than your fingernail, with bright orange spots that seem to glow in the dim light. This is the Adelphobates captivus, a species of poison dart frog that was only recently identified. Its brilliant colors warn predators that it's not safe to eat, a clever survival strategy that helps it thrive in the rainforest's dangerous ecosystem.

. . .

BUT NOT ALL discoveries are tiny. A few years ago, researchers stumbled upon a gigantic species of tarantula in the Amazon. Named Theraphosa blondi, or the Goliath bird-eating spider, this arachnid is as big as a dinner plate. Despite its terrifying size, it rarely eats birds—its diet mostly consists of insects, frogs, and small rodents. Finding such a massive spider was a reminder of how the rainforest can hide creatures that seem straight out of a science fiction movie.

THE RAINFOREST ISN'T JUST HOME to strange animals; its plants can be just as astonishing. One recent discovery is a type of orchid that blooms only at night. Found in the forests of Madagascar, this orchid emits a sweet fragrance after the sun goes down, attracting nocturnal pollinators like moths. Its petals are so delicate that they look like they could melt in your hand, yet this plant has managed to survive in the wild for centuries without anyone knowing it was there.

THEN THERE'S the glass frog, a creature so unusual it seems almost like a work of art. Its skin is translucent, meaning you can see its organs, including its beating heart, through its belly. Scientists discovered a new species of glass frog in Ecuador's rainforest, and its discovery made headlines around the world. What's even more remarkable is how little we still know about this frog's behavior and life cycle, showing just how many secrets the rainforest still holds.

NOT ALL DISCOVERIES happen deep in the forest. In some cases, scientists find new species right under their noses. For example, a previously unknown type of fungus was recently identified growing on leaves in the rainforest canopy. This fungus glows in the dark, emitting a soft green light that helps it attract insects, which spread its spores. Known as bioluminescence, this glowing ability is rare in fungi and has fascinated scientists studying its potential uses in medicine and technology.

FISH, too, are part of the rainforest's lineup of incredible discoveries. In the rivers of the Amazon, researchers recently found a new species of electric eel. Unlike other electric eels, this one can produce shocks of up to 860 volts—the most powerful electrical discharge ever recorded in an animal. Its discovery was a reminder of the raw, untamed power of the rainforest's wildlife.

. . .

SOME OF THE most exciting discoveries aren't about individual species but about how they interact with their environment. For instance, researchers have observed a type of ant that farms fungi. These ants cut pieces of leaves and carry them back to their nests, where they use the leaves to grow a specific type of fungus. This fungus becomes the ants' main food source, and the relationship between the ants and the fungus is so specialized that neither could survive without the other. It's like a tiny farming operation happening right on the forest floor.

ONE OF THE most heartwarming discoveries in recent years involved a new species of monkey in the Amazon. Named the Milton's titi monkey, this primate has a reddish-brown coat and a distinctive call. What makes it truly special is its social behavior. These monkeys are monogamous, meaning they form life-long bonds with their mates. They're often spotted sitting close together, their tails entwined—a touching reminder of the rainforest's many wonders.

EVEN INSECTS, which often go unnoticed, can be astonishing. In Papua New Guinea, scientists recently discovered a beetle so small that it could fit on the head of a pin. Despite its size, this beetle plays an important role in breaking down decaying plant material, helping to recycle nutrients back into the soil. It's proof that even the tiniest creatures can have a big impact on the ecosystem.

Strange and surprising phenomena

The rainforest is a place of endless surprises, where every rustle of leaves and every glimmer of light can hold a mystery waiting to be uncovered. Some of these mysteries are so strange that they feel like they belong in a fantasy story instead of real life. From trees that communicate to rivers that boil, the rainforest is full of phenomena that make you stop and wonder about the hidden powers of nature.

LET'S start with something that seems straight out of a science fiction movie—trees that talk to each other. While they don't speak with words, trees in the rainforest share information through an underground network of fungi known as mycorrhizae. Scientists sometimes call this the "wood wide web." Through this network, trees can send signals about things like drought or insect attacks, warning their neighbors to prepare. For example, if one tree is under attack by caterpillars, it can release chemicals that alert nearby trees to produce defensive toxins in their leaves. It's like the trees are whispering secrets to protect each other.

THE IDEA of talking trees is amazing, but it's just the beginning. Deep in the Amazon rainforest, there's a river that seems almost too dangerous to be real—the Boiling River. Located in Peru, this river is so hot that it can cook anything that falls into it. Its water reaches temperatures of up to 200 degrees Fahrenheit, and steam rises from its surface, making it look like a bubbling cauldron. The heat comes from geothermal energy beneath the Earth's surface. While the river is a beautiful sight, it's also a reminder of the raw power hidden in the rainforest.

ANOTHER STRANGE PHENOMENON involves the rainforest's rivers and their unpredictable behavior. During the rainy season, some rivers overflow their banks and flood the surrounding forest. But instead of destroying everything in their path, these floodwaters create a unique ecosystem called the varzea, or flooded forest. In this underwater world, fish like the pirarucu swim among tree trunks, and pink river dolphins play in the branches of submerged trees. It's like an enchanted version of the rainforest, where water takes over the land but life continues to thrive in surprising ways.

EVEN THE AIR in the rainforest holds mysteries. In some parts of the Amazon, you might see flashes of light that seem to come from nowhere. These are caused by bioluminescent insects, like fireflies, but the rainforest's versions are far more dramatic. Some insects emit a continuous glow, lighting up the forest like a magical lantern. Others flash in patterns, creating a mesmerizing light show that dances across the trees. Scientists believe these lights are used to attract mates or warn predators, but their beauty makes it easy to imagine they're part of a hidden magic.

THE RAINFOREST IS ALSO home to one of the most mysterious weather events on the planet—the morning mist. Each day, as the sun rises, a thick blanket of mist forms over the canopy, making the forest look like it's floating on a cloud. This mist isn't just beautiful; it's an important part of the rainforest's ecosystem. It helps trap heat and moisture, creating the perfect conditions for plants and animals to thrive. The mist also plays a role in forming clouds, which eventually bring rain back to the forest.

ONE OF THE strangest phenomena in the rainforest happens at night. When darkness falls, the forest comes alive with sounds, lights, and activity. Insects hum, frogs croak, and bats swoop through the trees. But what's truly surprising is the way some animals use sound to navigate and hunt. For example, certain types of bats use echolocation, sending out high-pitched sounds that bounce off objects and help them "see" in the dark. Even more amazing are the owls and jaguars, whose calls echo through the forest, adding to the mysterious symphony of the night.

SPEAKING OF NIGHT, there's a phenomenon called "green flash" that sometimes happens in the rainforest. It's a rare optical event where, just as the sun sets, a bright green light appears for a split second on the horizon. Scientists think it's caused by the way light bends as it passes through the atmosphere, but it's so fleeting that many people never get to see it. Those who do often describe it as magical, like the rainforest itself is winking at them.

. . .

ANOTHER ODDITY of the rainforest is the way it seems to create its own weather. The Amazon rainforest produces so much moisture that it generates rain clouds almost daily. This process begins with trees releasing water vapor through tiny openings in their leaves, a process called transpiration. As the vapor rises, it cools and condenses into clouds, eventually falling back to the forest as rain. It's like the rainforest is a self-sustaining water machine, constantly replenishing itself and the regions around it.

EVEN THE PLANTS in the rainforest can behave in ways that seem almost supernatural. There's a type of vine called the "strangler fig" that grows in a very unusual way. It starts as a tiny seed dropped by a bird or monkey onto the branch of another tree. From there, the vine grows downward, wrapping itself around the host tree's trunk. Over time, the vine grows thicker and stronger, sometimes completely taking over the host tree and replacing it. It's a dramatic and somewhat eerie reminder of the fierce competition for survival in the rainforest.

SOME PHENOMENA in the rainforest are still completely unexplained. For instance, there are reports of strange "singing" noises that seem to come from nowhere.

These sounds, sometimes described as low hums or whistles, have baffled scientists. Some believe they're caused by wind moving through certain tree formations, while others think they might be made by insects or other animals. Whatever the cause, these mysterious sounds add to the rainforest's sense of wonder and intrigue.

CONCLUSION

One reason the rainforest matters is because of the air we breathe. Trees are like nature's air filters, taking in carbon dioxide and releasing oxygen. The Amazon rainforest alone produces about 20% of the world's oxygen, which is why it's often called the "lungs of the Earth." Every breath you take is a reminder of how connected we are to these forests, even if you live far away from them. Without rainforests, the air wouldn't be as clean or as rich in oxygen, and the balance of gases in the atmosphere would be thrown off.

Rainforests also play a huge role in controlling the planet's climate. The trees and plants in the rainforest store massive amounts of carbon dioxide, keeping it out of the atmosphere and helping to slow down global warming. But when forests are cut down or burned, that carbon is released back into the air, making climate change worse. By protecting rain-forests, we're not just saving trees; we're helping to keep the Earth's temperature steady and creating a healthier planet for everyone.

Water is another reason the rainforest is impor-tant. Rainforests are like giant sponges, absorbing rain and releasing it slowly into rivers and streams. The Amazon River, which flows through the heart of the rainforest, is the largest river in the world by volume. It provides water for millions of people, as well as countless animals and plants. The rainforest also creates its own weather, releasing water vapor into the air that eventually falls back as rain. This cycle keeps the rainforest lush and green, but it also affects weather patterns far beyond South America. Farmers in the United States, for example, depend on the Amazon's rain cycle to grow their crops.

Beyond air and water, the rainforest matters because of the incredible variety of life it holds. Every species in the rainforest, no matter how small, plays a role in keeping the ecosystem balanced. Bees and butterflies pollinate plants, which feed animals and produce seeds for new trees. Predators like jaguars keep herbivore populations in check, preventing them from overgrazing. And fungi break down dead plants and animals, recycling nutrients back into the soil. This web of life is so complex and interconnected that losing even one piece of it can affect the entire system.

Many of the foods we eat and products we use come from the rainforest. Bananas, chocolate, vanilla, and coffee all have their origins in tropical forests. Medicines, too, owe a lot to the rainforest. Scientists have found compounds in rainforest plants that are used to treat diseases like cancer, malaria, and heart disease. But only a fraction of the rainforest's plants have been studied, which means there could be countless other cures waiting to be discovered.

The rainforest is also home to people who have lived there for generations. Indigenous communities have deep connections to the land, relying on the forest for food, shelter, and medicine. Their traditional knowledge of the rainforest's plants and animals is invaluable, helping scientists understand and protect this complex ecosystem. Supporting these communities is another way to protect the rainforest, as their sustainable way of living keeps the forest healthy and thriving.

Even if you've never been to a rainforest, its survival impacts your daily life. The coffee you drink in the morning, the oxygen you breathe, the weather patterns that bring rain to your town—all of these are connected to the rainforest. Protecting it isn't just about saving a distant, faraway place; it's about ensuring that the planet as a whole can continue to support life.

The rainforest also inspires us. Its towering trees,

colorful birds, and mysterious creatures remind us of how amazing the natural world can be. It's a place that sparks curiosity and wonder, encouraging people to explore, learn, and care about the environment. The more we learn about the rainforest, the more we realize how much it has to teach us—not just about science, but about our own place in the world.

Every action we take to protect the rainforest, no matter how small, makes a difference. Recycling, choosing sustainable products, and raising awareness are all ways we can help. By working together, we can ensure that the rainforest remains a thriving, vital part of our planet, not just for the animals and plants that live there, but for all of us who depend on its gifts.

The rainforest matters to everyone because it's more than just a forest. It's a source of life, a protector of the planet, and a reminder of how incredible the world can be when we take care of it.

APPENDIX

Glossary

Biodiversity

Biodiversity is like a giant treasure chest filled with every kind of living thing you can imagine—plants, animals, fungi, and even tiny microorganisms. The rainforest is one of the most biodiverse places on Earth, meaning it has more different types of life than almost anywhere else. This variety is what makes the rainforest so special. Think of it this way: a rainforest with high biodiversity is like a big, colorful puzzle where every piece fits together perfectly. Each species, no matter how small, plays a role in keeping the ecosystem healthy.

Why does biodiversity matter? Imagine if one piece of that puzzle disappeared, like a bee that helps pollinate flowers. Without the bee, plants might not grow as well, which could affect the animals that eat those plants. Everything is connected, and biodiversity is what keeps those connections strong.

Canopy

The canopy is the rainforest's upper layer, a vast green roof made of tree branches and leaves. This layer is where much of the action happens in the rainforest. Monkeys leap between the branches, toucans search for fruit, and insects buzz through the leaves. The canopy is so dense that only a small amount of sunlight reaches the layers below, creating a cooler, darker world on the forest floor.

Picture the canopy as the rainforest's bustling city. It's filled with life and movement, and it provides food and shelter for countless creatures. Some plants, like epiphytes, even grow directly on the branches of canopy trees, getting all the sunlight and moisture they need without ever touching the ground.

Ecosystem

An ecosystem is like a big, interconnected family where every member depends on the others. It's made up of all the living things in a particular area, like plants, animals, and fungi, plus the non-living things they rely on, such as water, sunlight, and soil. The rainforest is one giant ecosystem, but it's also full of smaller ecosystems, like rivers, swamps, and forest floors.

In an ecosystem, every part plays a role. A tree provides oxygen for animals to breathe, and when it falls, it becomes a home for fungi and insects. Those insects might become food for birds, which spread seeds that grow into new trees. It's a cycle where nothing is wasted, and everything has a purpose.

Emergent Layer

The emergent layer is the very top of the rainforest, where the tallest trees reach above the canopy. These trees, like the majestic kapok tree, can grow over 200 feet tall, towering above everything else. This layer gets the most sunlight and is often windy, making it the perfect home for eagles, bats, and some adventurous monkeys.

Imagine the emergent layer as the skyscrapers of the rainforest, standing high above the rest of the forest. These trees are the giants of the rainforest, and they play a vital role in producing oxygen and providing shelter for animals that prefer life at great heights.

Understory

The understory is the layer beneath the canopy, a shadowy, quieter part of the rainforest. This is where you'll find jaguars, snakes, and many insects hiding among the leaves. The understory is also home to smaller plants that don't need much sunlight, like ferns and orchids.

If the canopy is the city of the rainforest, the

understory is like its quiet neighborhoods, full of secrets and surprises. It's a great place for animals that want to stay hidden, whether they're hunting or avoiding being hunted.

Forest Floor

The forest floor is where the rainforest meets the ground. It's a dark, damp place, but it's full of life. This is where fungi break down dead plants and animals, recycling nutrients back into the soil. It's also home to larger animals like tapirs and armadillos, as well as tiny decomposers like ants and termites.

The forest floor might seem less glamorous than the canopy or the emergent layer, but it's just as important. It's like the foundation of a house—without it, the rainforest couldn't survive.

Photosynthesis

Photosynthesis is the process plants use to make their own food. They take in sunlight, carbon dioxide, and water and turn them into energy, releasing oxygen as a byproduct. This process is what makes plants so special—they don't need to hunt for food like animals do.

In the rainforest, photosynthesis is happening everywhere, from the smallest fern on the forest floor to the tallest tree in the emergent layer. This process is what fills the rainforest with oxygen, making it a crucial part of our planet's air supply.

Rain Cycle

The rain cycle is the process that keeps the rainforest, well, rainy! Water evaporates from the leaves of trees and rises into the atmosphere, where it cools and turns into clouds. Eventually, the water falls back to the forest as rain, starting the cycle all over again.

This cycle is what makes rainforests so lush and green. It also helps regulate the climate, not just in the rainforest but all over the world.

Deforestation

Deforestation means cutting down trees and clearing land, often to make room for farms, roads, or buildings. While humans need these things, deforestation can be harmful when it happens too quickly or in the wrong places. It destroys habitats, reduces biodiversity, and releases carbon dioxide into the atmosphere.

Understanding deforestation is important because it reminds us of the choices we can make to help protect the rainforest. Supporting sustainable products and reforestation projects are ways we can help reduce its impact.

Sustainable

Sustainable means using resources in a way that doesn't harm the environment or use them up completely. For example, sustainable farming practices might involve planting crops without cutting down too many trees or using renewable energy sources like solar power instead of fossil fuels.

When something is sustainable, it's like planting a garden—you're taking what you need while making sure there's more for the future.

Carbon Dioxide

Carbon dioxide is a gas that animals exhale and plants absorb during photosynthesis. It's a natural part of the air, but too much of it can trap heat in the atmosphere, causing global warming.

Rainforests act like giant sponges for carbon dioxide, absorbing it and helping to keep the planet's temperature steady. This makes them one of our best allies in fighting climate change.

Fun Activities

How to create a mini rainforest terrarium at home

Have you ever dreamed of bringing the rainforest into your home? While you can't exactly move a whole rainforest into your room, you can create your own tiny version of one—a mini rainforest terrarium. It's like having a piece of the wild, humid forest right on your windowsill. Plus, building a terrarium is not just fun; it's a great way to learn about ecosystems and how plants grow in the rainforest's unique conditions.

Let's dive in and explore how to make your own little rainforest world step by step. By the end, you'll have your very own green masterpiece to admire and care for.

What You'll Need

Creating a mini rainforest terrarium doesn't require fancy tools or rare items. Most of the materials can be found at home, in a garden store, or even outside. Here's what you'll need:

- **A clear container**: A glass jar, old aquarium, or even a plastic soda bottle cut in half can work. It needs a lid to keep the moisture inside, mimicking the rainforest's humidity.
- **Gravel or small rocks**: These will form the base layer to help with drainage.
- **Activated charcoal**: This is optional but helps keep the terrarium fresh and prevents odors.
- **Potting soil**: Choose soil that's light and rich, similar to what plants would find in the rainforest.
- **Small plants**: Look for plants that love moisture and indirect light, like ferns, moss, or small tropical plants.
- **Decorations**: Miniature figurines, pretty stones, or tiny logs can make your terrarium look even more magical.

- **Spray bottle:** This will help you mist your terrarium to keep it nice and humid.

Once you've gathered your supplies, it's time to get creative!

Step-by-Step Instructions
Step 1: Prepare Your Container

Start by cleaning your container to make sure it's free of dust and dirt. A clear container will let you see all the layers of your terrarium, just like peeling back the rainforest's layers to see what's happening inside. If you're using a jar with a lid, you're already set. If you're using an open container, you can cover it later with plastic wrap to trap moisture.

Step 2: Add a Layer of Rocks

Spread a layer of small rocks or gravel at the bottom of your container. This is the foundation of your terrarium and will help water drain away from the soil, preventing your plants from getting water-logged. Think of it as the forest floor, which absorbs rain but doesn't let water puddle up.

Step 3: Sprinkle Activated Charcoal

If you have activated charcoal, sprinkle a thin layer over the rocks. This step helps filter the water and keeps everything smelling fresh. It's like giving your terrarium a built-in air purifier.

Step 4: Add the Soil

Now it's time to add the soil. Scoop enough potting

soil to create a layer about two to three inches thick. This is where your plants will grow, just like they would in the rich, nutrient-filled soil of the rainforest. Use your hands or a spoon to gently level the soil and remove any big clumps.

Step 5: Choose and Plant Your Greenery

Here comes the fun part—planting! Select small plants that will fit comfortably in your container. Moss, small ferns, and baby tropical plants are all great choices. Carefully dig small holes in the soil, place your plants in them, and cover the roots with soil. Arrange the plants however you like—grouping them can create the feeling of a mini rainforest grove.

If you're using moss, gently press it onto the soil's surface. Moss doesn't have roots, so it just needs to be in contact with the moist soil to thrive.

Step 6: Decorate Your Rainforest

This is where you get to make your rainforest unique. Add tiny rocks, twigs, or little animal figurines to your terrarium. You might even want to create a path using pebbles or a "river" with blue glass beads. These decorations don't just make your terrarium look cool—they also help tell a story about what's happening in your mini rainforest.

Step 7: Water and Close

Using your spray bottle, lightly mist the plants and soil. You want the soil to be damp but not soaking wet, just like the rainforest after a gentle rain. Once your terrarium is watered, close the lid or cover it with plastic wrap to trap the moisture inside. This will create a humid environment that mimics the rainforest's climate.

Caring for Your Mini Rainforest

Now that your terrarium is built, it's time to keep it healthy and happy. Place it in a spot with indirect sunlight—too much direct sun can make it too hot inside the container. Check on your terrarium every few days. If the soil looks dry, give it a light misting. If water starts collecting at the bottom, open the lid for a while to let some moisture escape.

Over time, you might notice condensation forming on the inside of the container. This is a good sign—it means your mini rainforest is creating its own water cycle, just like the real rainforest!

Why It's More Than Just a Craft

Building a terrarium isn't just about creating something beautiful; it's a way to see how ecosystems work. Inside your terrarium, plants, water, and air interact in a closed environment. The plants take in carbon dioxide and release oxygen, and the water cycle keeps the soil moist. It's like a tiny version of the rainforest, showing you how every part of the system works together.

Your terrarium is also a reminder of how delicate nature can be. The rainforest is much bigger and more complex than your mini version, but it relies on the same careful balance to survive. By caring for your terrarium, you're practicing the skills needed to care for the larger natural world.

Rainforest trivia quiz

Easy Questions

Let's begin with some questions to get you warmed up:

1. **What is the largest rainforest in the world?**
   - a) The Congo Rainforest
   - b) The Amazon Rainforest
   - c) The Daintree Rainforest
   - d) The Borneo Rainforest
2. *Hint: It's so big that it spans nine countries!*
3. **Which layer of the rainforest is called the "roof"?**
   - a) Emergent Layer
   - b) Canopy
   - c) Understory
   - d) Forest Floor
4. *Hint: This layer is home to toucans and monkeys.*
5. **What percentage of Earth's oxygen is produced by rainforests?**
   - a) 10%

- ○ b) 20%
- ○ c) 50%
- ○ d) 70%

6. *Hint: It's why rainforests are sometimes called the "lungs of the Earth."*

7. **Which rainforest animal is known for its bright colors and toxic skin?**
   - ○ a) Sloth
   - ○ b) Poison Dart Frog
   - ○ c) Jaguar
   - ○ d) Anteater

8. *Hint: Its colors are a warning sign to predators!*

9. **What type of water lily has leaves big enough to hold a small child?**
   - ○ a) Amazon Lily
   - ○ b) Victoria amazonica
   - ○ c) Giant Lotus
   - ○ d) Tropical Water Lily

10. *Hint: These leaves can grow over six feet wide.*

Medium Questions

Now that you're warmed up, let's make things a little more challenging:

1. **How many layers does a rainforest have?**
   - ○ a) Two
   - ○ b) Three
   - ○ c) Four

- d) Five
2. *Hint: Think of the canopy, but don't forget the other layers!*
3. **What is the name of the underground network that trees use to "communicate"?**
   - a) Root system
   - b) Mycorrhizal network
   - c) Soil web
   - d) Fungal thread
4. *Hint: Some call it the "wood wide web."*
5. **Which river runs through the Amazon Rainforest?**
   - a) Nile
   - b) Ganges
   - c) Amazon
   - d) Mississippi
6. *Hint: It's the second-longest river in the world.*
7. **Which rainforest bird has a large, colorful beak?**
   - a) Macaw
   - b) Toucan
   - c) Parrot
   - d) Cockatoo
8. *Hint: Its beak is as bright as a rainbow!*
9. **What is the primary reason rainforests are being cut down?**
   - a) Farming
   - b) Tourism

- c) Wildfires
- d) Mining

10. *Hint: Think of palm oil and cattle ranching.*

Hard Questions

Think you're ready to tackle the toughest questions? Let's see how much you really know:

1. **What is the tallest tree species found in rainforests?**
   - a) Kapok Tree
   - b) Mahogany Tree
   - c) Brazil Nut Tree
   - d) Ceiba Tree
2. *Hint: These giants can grow over 200 feet tall.*
3. **What is the name of the rare glowing fungi found in rainforests?**
   - a) Bioluminescent Mushroom
   - b) Ghost Fungus
   - c) Firefly Fungus
   - d) Neon Spore
4. *Hint: It emits a greenish light in the dark.*
5. **What is the term for plants that grow on trees without harming them?**
   - a) Epiphytes
   - b) Parasites
   - c) Lianas
   - d) Saprophytes

6. *Hint: Orchids and bromeliads are examples.*

7. **Which rainforest creature is often called the "gardener of the forest"?**
   - a) Jaguar
   - b) Leafcutter Ant
   - c) Tapir
   - d) Sloth

8. *Hint: This animal spreads seeds as it moves through the forest.*

9. **What is the boiling river in Peru called?**
   - a) Río Caliente
   - b) Shanay-Timpishka
   - c) Agua Ardiente
   - d) Río Fuego

10. *Hint: Its name means "heated by the sun" in a local language.*

Answers and Fun Facts

Let's check how many you got right:

1. **b) The Amazon Rainforest**

2. *Fun Fact: The Amazon is so large that it's often called the "Green Ocean."*

3. **b) Canopy**

4. *Fun Fact: The canopy is so dense that only about 2% of sunlight reaches the forest floor.*

5. **b) 20%**

6. *Fun Fact: Rainforests play a huge role in producing the oxygen we breathe every day.*

7. **b) Poison Dart Frog**

8. *Fun Fact: Indigenous people used the frog's toxins to coat their hunting darts.*

9. **b) Victoria amazonica**

10. *Fun Fact: This giant water lily is named after Queen Victoria of England.*

11. **c) Four**

12. *Fun Fact: The layers are emergent, canopy, understory, and forest floor.*

13. **b) Mycorrhizal network**

14. *Fun Fact: This underground fungal network helps trees share nutrients and warnings.*

15. **c) Amazon**

16. *Fun Fact: During the rainy season, the Amazon River can grow to over 30 miles wide.*

17. **b) Toucan**

18. *Fun Fact: A toucan's beak might look heavy, but it's surprisingly light and strong.*

19. **a) Farming**

20. *Fun Fact: Agriculture, especially palm oil plantations and cattle ranching, is a major cause of deforestation.*

21. **a) Kapok Tree**

22. *Fun Fact: The kapok tree is also known as the silk-cotton tree because of the fluffy fibers in its seeds.*

23. **a) Bioluminescent Mushroom**

24. *Fun Fact: These glowing fungi attract insects, which help spread their spores.*

25. **a) Epiphytes**

26. *Fun Fact: Epiphytes don't take nutrients from the trees they live on—they gather them from the air and rain.*

27. **c) Tapir**

28. *Fun Fact: Tapirs are excellent swimmers and help keep rainforest ecosystems thriving by spreading seeds.*

29. **b) Shanay-Timpishka**

30. *Fun Fact: The boiling river is so hot that it can literally cook small animals that fall into it.*

Made in United States
Troutdale, OR
04/22/2025